out of print A2

ISLAM IN CENTRAL ASIA

ISLAM IN CENTRAL ASIA

Ludmila Polonskaya
and
Alexei Malashenko

Ithaca Press
Reading, 1994

© Garnet Publishing 1994

First English edition

ISBN 0 86372 182 6

British Library Cataloguing-in-Publication Data
A catalogue record for this book is available from the British Library

Jacket design by David Rose
Typeset by Columns Design & Production Services Limited, Reading

Printed in Lebanon

Ithaca Press is an imprint of Garnet Publishing Ltd,
8 Southern Court, Southe Street, Reading, RG1 4QS

CONTENTS

LIST OF ILLUSTRATIONS

CHAPTER ONE

ISLAM AND CENTRAL ASIA BEFORE THE RUSSIAN CONQUEST

Central Asia at the crossroads of the greatest cultures of antiquity

The religious situation in pre-Islamic times

In pre-Islamic times, Central Asia was a region where the greatest cultures of antiquity met and interacted. The region was largely similar to pre-Islamic Arabia. In the first place, both areas were characterised by active interaction and mutual alienation between the cultures of nomadic and settled ethnic groups. Long before Islam came into being, people leading a settled way of life developed psychological stereotypes that made them regard their nomadic neighbours as potential enemies. This influenced the spread of Islam and was mirrored in that religion.

Another feature common to Central Asia and Arabia was the importance of trade. The *Silk Route* – a major Oriental trade route between China and West Asia – ran across Central Asia. The effect of the *Silk Route* on the development and interaction of regional cultures can hardly be overestimated.

Many typological features of pre-Islamic Central Asian and Arab societies are clearly similar. However, there are significant differences between Arabia – the birthplace of the Islamic world – and Central Asia, an outlying part of that world. On joining the Moslem world, Central Asia brought with it local cultural features, creating a special type of Islamic civilisation. For this, there were several reasons.

By the time Islam emerged, the Arab ethnic group already existed in Arabia. In Central Asia, multi-ethnic societies were developing. Like Arabia, Central Asia formed part of several large empires in ancient times and in the early Middle Ages. But a few separate states were established in the region in pre-Islamic times.

In the early seventh century, Central Asia was the scene of wars between the Turki Khaganate (which existed from AD 552 to 745) and Sasanid Iran. Most of Central Asia was part of the Khaganate, whose core was a federation of ten large Turki tribes. The Khagan had supreme sovereignty over the conquered peoples, but nomadic tribes of the Khaganate and even small states that had emerged in permanent-population areas were relatively independent and were governed by local rulers. The largest of these states were Sogdiana, Bukhara, Usrushana, Fergana, Termez, and Tahiristan. The name Sogdiana applied to several small principalities whose rulers were of the Kan dynasty, the most important being the Sogdiana of Samarkand. Bukhara comprised several small possessions governed by the ruler of Bukhara proper. Usrushana comprised a territory known as Chach with a town called Binkent (now Tashkent). Sogdiana was followed in size and importance by Tahiristan, which comprised what is now the southern part of Tajikistan, the Surkhan Darya Region of Uzbekistan, and the north of Afghanistan. For a long time, large parts of Tahiristan, Sogdiana, and other territories in southern Central Asia, with urban, rural, and nomadic populations, were parts of Sasanid Iran. But by the time of the Arab conquest, Iran retained only a few areas in what is now southern Turkmenia.

Ancient religions

There were centres of major religious cultures in ancient Central Asia. Pagan cults were quite common (as they were in pre-Islamic Arabia), but Zoroastrianism, Buddhism, and Manichaeism were also widespread.

The founder of the most ancient religion, Zarathustra (known to Europeans as Zoroaster, the name meaning 'camel driver'), lived in the late seventh and the early sixth centuries BC; legend has it that he lived in Central Asia or in adjacent territories. Most of his followers were in Central Asia. Later parts of the *Avesta* – Zoroastrianism's holy book – describe Central Asian societies. That is evident from the geographical zones and the countries mentioned.

Zarathustra rejected earlier tribal cults, worshipped Ahura Mazda as the only god, but regarded Good and Evil as two eternal mutually opposed elements. As the religious system of Zoroastrianism developed after Zarathustra's death, the monotheistic trend and dualism remained. At the same time, Zoroastrianism was adapted to local pagan cults. And, although no syncretic religions ever evolved in Central Asia, syncretic trends were always strong in the region. Zoroastrians always regarded life as a gift from the good element and death as evil – hence the Zoroastrian burial ceremony: corpses were put on a platform to be devoured by carrion-eating birds and the bones were preserved in special vessels. In Central Asia, however, the rite did not become widespread. Deaths were mourned there, although mourning was prohibited by Zoroastrian religious texts. Descriptions of mourning rites are found in *Shah-Nameh* (a collection of poetic and prosaic myths and chronicles of Persian-speaking peoples) and in Sogdian fine arts.

In Sogdiana, Zoroastrianism coexisted with the cult of Dessi in pre-Islamic times. The spirit was represented as a gold idol. It was customary to kill five camels, ten horses, and 100 sheep as a sacrifice to Dessi.

Worship of the forces of nature and shamanism were also widespread throughout Central Asia. The most important deity was the 'spirit of the blue sky' ('kok tengri'). In Samarkand there existed the cult of a divine babe, associated with worship of a god who died and was reborn again.

Pagan cults coexisted with Zoroastrian worship of the elements, especially of fire, and fire-worshippers' temples stood next to pagan sanctuaries.

Some scholars believe that Central Asia's Zoroastrianism is quite different from the classical religion and that, in Central Asia, Zoroastrianism closely synthesised with paganism, creating what can be regarded as a syncretic Sogdian religion, and that religion has been termed Mazdaism.

Another important source of Central Asia's religious culture in pre-Islamic times was Buddhism. Although some Chinese travellers wrote in the sixth and early seventh centuries that Sogdiana's 'king and people do not believe in Buddha but worship fire', the pre-Islamic religious traditions of Sogdiana proper – and especially of Tahiristan – were clearly influenced by Buddhism.

This religion began to spread in the region at the time of the Achaemenids, but specific sources with information about its establishment in Central Asia date from a later period. Buddhism came by way of Afghanistan and advanced in two directions – westwards, to Merv and eastern Pathia, and eastwards, to Termez and Bashkiria. According to chronicles of those times a famous Central Asian scholar came to Lo-yang in the year 148 and began to translate Buddhist books into Chinese, which was how Buddhism entered China.

Many interesting facts are known about other Buddhist preachers: Ghoshak (who was born in Tahiristan) and Dharmamitra (a native of Termez). The prevailing Buddhist school in Central Asia was Vaibhashika. By the time Islam came to the region, there were Buddhists in Tahiristan and Sogdiana and among the Turkis. In the early seventh century, there were about 100 Buddhist monasteries in Balkh and about ten in Termez while other towns in Central Asia had two or three each. Parkhar, the administrative centre of a district in the lower reaches of the Kizyl River in southern Tajikistan, got its name, linguists say, from the Sanskrit word *vihara*, meaning 'a Buddhist monastery'. Buddhist birch-bark manuscripts have been found in Namazga-Tepe and Buddhism found its way even into the Pamirs.

Another religion that existed in Central Asia up to the Islamic era was Manichaeism. Although its fundamental concept of the conflict of two eternal principles, good and evil, had much in common with Zoroastrian ideas, the adherents of Manichaeism were persecuted by Zoroastrians. Manichaeism was professed by several rulers and noblemen of Tahiristan. The religion contributed to the development of prophetism in Central Asia, for Mani, the founder of Manichaeism, was venerated as the Comforter from the heavenly world of light. So by the time Islam came to Central Asia, people there were already acquainted with the idea of prophetism.

Early arrival of Christianity

Historically, Islam was not the first monotheistic religion in Central Asia. Christianity, mainly Nestorianism, had already found its way there. Theophylactus Simokatta and Theophanus of Byzantium wrote that some Turkis in the army of Bahram Chubin, the famous Sasanid military leader of the latter half of the sixth century, had crosses cut on their foreheads. Turki women cut crosses on their children's foreheads hoping that these would protect them from disease. Nestorianism was adopted by many Turki rulers in Tahiristan and they sent Nestorian delegations to other regions for missionary work.[1]

This shows that before Islam found its way into Central Asia and became established there, there were various religious sources contributing to the development of the people's world outlook, psychology, lifestyles, and mentality. The merging of the cultures of nomadic and settled ethnic groups was far from complete, and the process was complicated by an intricate interaction of various religious traditions which directly influenced another process that took place in that period – the development of ethnoses.

From the seventh and the sixth centuries BC, the territory now known as Central Asia was inhabited by tribes belonging to the Iranian ethnic group. The area was their ancient, but not original, habitat. Central Asia was the region from which they spread to other areas. Iranian ethnoses and Turki ethnic components later provided a basis for the development of modern peoples of Central Asia – the Tajik, the Uzbek, the Turkomans, the Kirghiz, and the Kazakh. This is illustrated by ancient written documents and by historico-linguistic and archaeological research. Some peoples (such as the Tajik) were influenced in their genesis mainly by Iranian elements, others (the Uzbek, the Turkomans, etc.), by Turki elements.

Central Asia was a crossroads where various cultures and civilisations came together, and that was reflected in the region's entire social development. Before Islam found its way into Central Asia, the region had known a great variety of interacting religious trends, from paganism and cosmic religion (Hinduism, Buddhism) to religious syncretism or clear-cut monotheism. Monotheism was incarnated in Islam, so the youngest monotheistic religion soon became the prevailing religion of Central Asia.

Why did Islam succeed?

The establishment of Islam in Central Asia was helped greatly by wars which led to most of the region being incorporated into the Arab Caliphate. On many occasions in history, however, a religion imposed on conquered peoples by force has failed to take root, and coercion has only enhanced adherence to local beliefs. Islam, in contrast, developed from the invaders' religion into Central Asia's pre-eminent religion in less than a century.

The conquest of the territory between the Amu Darya and the Syr Darya (formerly Sogdiana), which the Arabs called *Ma Wara al-Nahr* (meaning 'that which [lies] beyond the river' in Arabic), began in the third quarter of the seventh century. Khorasan was conquered in 644 and served as a bridgehead for campaigns across the Amu Darya. The first Arab army to cross the river was led by Ubaydallah ibn Ziyad, Caliph Muawiya's governor in Iraq. He conquered and ravaged the area around Bukhara. After fierce fighting with a united Turki-Bukhara army, he had to conclude peace with the regent of Bukhara who is known in history as 'Takhshada's mother'. (Takhshada was the ruler of Bukhara during the Arab conquest.)

Under the peace treaty, the Arabs took a great amount of gold and silver coins away to Khorasan, together with piles of well-crafted weapons and about 4,000 prisoners. But peace did not last long. In 676 Bukhara was besieged by the Arab governor of Khorasan, Said ibn Osman. Bukhara's allies – the rulers of Sogdiana, Kesh and Nesef – pulled their troops out of the war and the regent of Bukhara (Takhshada's mother) was forced to accept an extremely humiliating peace treaty. She paid 300,000 dirhams to the Arab leader, and the Arabs took as hostages 80 young noblemen of Bukhara, including members of the sovereign family. The Arab governor promised to release the hostages as soon as he crossed the Amu Darya on his way back to Khorasan, but he did not keep his word; instead, he sent them away to Arabia to work in his possessions there as slaves. According to

Narshakhi's *History of Bukhara,* the freedom-loving and warlike Bukharans refused to tolerate such humiliation. A group of Bukharans forced their way into Said ibn-Osman's palace and killed him, then killed themselves.[2]

That is just one episode illustrating Central Asia's first reaction to the Arab invasion. The subsequent history of the Arab conquest is full of dramatic events. It took Arab warlord Qutaybah ibn Muslim (in the early eighth century) ten years to conquer *Ma Wara al-Nahr.*

The region's political fragmentation and religious division, the conflicts between the Western Turki Khaganate and China over territories in Central Asia, and constant internecine wars waged among local rulers all made the Arabs' victory easier. While the people of *Ma Wara al-Nahr* displayed real heroism in resisting the invaders, some merchants and noblemen sided with the invaders against their own people. The Arab leader's superior strength and great skill were supplemented by diplomatic abilities; he was cruel against those who put up resistance and tried to win over people who could help the Arabs to consolidate their rule, such as local sovereigns, merchants, and educated people.

Arab historian al-Tabari writes about a loan taken by the Arab governor of Koharasan from Sogdian merchants as early as the end of the seventh century (in 696). Some merchants did collaborate with the Arabs during Qutaybah's conquests. But most people fought hard against the Arabs for a long time. Arab and Persian sources present a dramatic picture of the capture of Paikend, known as 'a town of merchants' or 'the Copper Town'. (Like Samarkand, it was one of the most ancient towns of *Ma Wara al-Nahr.*) After Qutaybah captured the town, signed a peace treaty with its ruler and moved his forces back to the Amu Darya, there was an uprising in Paikend and the Arab occupation force was wiped out. Qutaybah recaptured the town in a siege that lasted a whole month. The Arabs then took great treasures and many weapons. Qutaybah distributed the weapons among his soldiers and ordered that the gold and silver vessels and gold idols be melted down and that the people of Paikend gather and watch the melting. The people were certain that their deities would immediately bring down cruel retribution on the invaders. But nothing happened.

When most of Central Asia had been captured, Samarkand remained the only town still fighting the Arabs. At one point, its ruler Tarkhun, wishing to avoid bloodshed, agreed to pay tribute to the Arabs, but was deposed by his own people. The newly elected ruler, Gurek, refused to submit to the Arabs. Qutaybah could not move his forces against Samarkand until he had completely subdued Bukhara and Khorezm. Bukhara was taken by storm as was Khorezm, through a deal with its ruler, the Khorezm Shah. In 711, in the face of an uprising led by his own brother, the Khorezm Shah requested help from Qutaybah, sending him the golden keys to the town's gate. The Arab warlord helped the Khorezm Shah to suppress the uprising; the ruler's mutinous brother was killed, but Khorezm submitted to the Arab ruler. Troops of Khorezm, as well as Bukhara, helped the Arabs to conquer other territories in Central Asia, starting with Samarkand.

Conquest of Samarkand

The rulers of Shasha and Fergana, not yet conquered by the Arabs, sent their best forces to help Samarkand. Samarkand's ruler Gurek added those forces to his own and moved his army to rebuff the enemy. The decisive battle was fought outside the walls of Samarkand. At first the forces defending the town were more successful, but the Arabs overwhelmed them, using 300 battering machines, and captured the town.[3]

Under the peace treaty then concluded, the rulers of Samarkand were obliged to pay an annual tribute of 2,200,000 dirhams to the Arabs as well as to pull their troops out of the inner town and to allow Qutaybah to build a mosque in Samarkand. On Qutaybah's orders, they brought all the treasures from the Fire Temple, as well as gold and silver ornaments and idols, to a designated place. According to al-Tabari, the pile was as big as a castle. As in Paikend, Qutaybah ordered that the gold be melted down. Gurek and other Sogdians begged the Arabs not do do this, warning that their sacrilege would be punished, but Qutaybah himself threw the first log to make the fire. The gold was melted down; it totalled 50,000 zolotniks[4] (about 213.3 kilograms). There was no divine punishment this time, either. The Arabs built a mosque and it functioned safely – which clearly demonstrated the supremacy of the new religion.

The local population was led increasingly to believe that the Arabs were winning wars because they worshipped the only real god, Allah, while their own deities failed to united or protect them from the invaders.

Islam came to *Ma Wara al-Nahr* with Arab military leaders, Arab troops stationed there, Arab nomads and even farmers who moved to the region after the conquest. But it would be wrong to say that Islam was a religion imposed on the region by the Arab conquerors and their rulers. Islam was not established in Central Asia by force only. The new religion was popularised by Moslem merchants who moved to the Arab Caliphate's newly acquired territories. And the First Moslem missionaries in Central Asia, as well as in many other regions and countries, were Sufis.

It was an extremely important factor that at its very outset, and later, as it spread to other regions, Islam was able to absorb certain social institutions and local religious ideas that were deeply embedded in the local mentality.

Central Asia was incorporated into the Arab Caliphate at a time when the establishment of Islam as a religion was not yet complete. An important contribution to Islam's development was made by Persian theologians living in Iran and in what is now Central Asia, which explains why Islam absorbed many of the ideas that were widespread there at the time.

It became obvious that there was much in common between certain Zoroastrian and Islamic ideas even before Islam was brought to Central Asia, during the Arab conquest of Iran. The similarity is especially obvious if one looks at the eschatology of Islam. Like Zoroastrianism, Islam says that in the afterlife a person's soul will suffer or rejoice, depending on the person's behaviour on Earth. The concept of *Sirat* – a bridge spanning Hell and leading to Heaven (in Islam, it is the only road to Heaven) – stems from Zoroastrian beliefs, too. Other common features include performance of divine worship five times a day, the concept of ritual purity, and the selection of Friday as the day of weekly gathering.

It is a well-known fact that Islam has much in common with Christianity and Judaism also. These points in common include the very idea of monotheism, the veneration of biblical persons as the greatest prophets, etc.

So when it found its way into Central Asia, Islam was not seen there as an utterly alien religion. This does not mean, however, that Islam established itself in the region without opposing other religions or that it completely absorbed other religions in the process. As it did everywhere, Islam acted against other religions in Central Asia. Moslems regarded Central Asia's pre-Islamic religions as *jahiliyya* ('lack of faith, infidelity'), although many local rites were legalised by Islam.

Seventh-century rebellion

Local cults retained their isolation from, and hostility to, Islam. Many promoted anti-feudal rebellions in the first century following the inclusion of Central Asia in the Arab Caliphate. For example, Mukannah, who led a major anti-Arab uprising in the latter half of the seventh century, advocated religious views strongly influenced by Mazdakism (a teaching close to Manichaeism which was the ideology of popular movements against the exploitative classes in the late fifth and early sixth centuries. Mukannah's slogans reflected the ideas of God's embodiment as man and of transmigration of souls. He sent letters throughout *Ma Wara al-Nahr* telling people that he was the God Incarnate of Adam, Noah, Moses, Abraham, Jesus, and Muhammad and that 'everyone who joined him would go to heaven, and those who acted against him would go to hell'. The whole of *Ma Wara al-Nahr* was caught up in Mukannah's uprising. Both settled peasants and nomads joined Mukannah; he was supported even by Bukhar-Khudat Buniat ibn-Takhshad, who rejected Islam and was eager to restore Bukhara's independence. The uprising is known in history as 'the white-robed men's movement'. According to al-Biruni, it lasted 14 years, and some protests by 'white-robed men' took place even in the twelfth century.[5]

Undoubtedly, the conquest of Central Asia by the Arabs and the endless wars and uprisings in the seventh and eighth centuries caused a decline of material and spiritual culture in the region. But the decline was temporary. Many Russian and Central Asian scholars justly believed that – looked at in the light of subsequent events – the inclusion of Central Asia in the Arab Caliphate and the establishment of Islam there promoted the consolidation of Central Asia's peoples and helped to overcome fragmentation and build centralised states, and that that provided better conditions for the development of modern ethnic groups. Central Asia's social development featured 'a great cultural synthesis'.[6]

The principal eternal values, guidelines, and precepts laid down in the Koran were adopted by Central Asian societies. That was largely because Islam, closely linked with social development and politics from the very outset, was the most down-to-earth and pragmatic of all the religions known in Central Asia. But most importantly, by adapting the local spiritual substratum, Islam acquired specific features in Central Asia which make it quite different from Islam as it exists in the Arab world and in other historico-cultural regions.

The process was formalised as Central Asia developed its own system of religious authorities, different from the Arab one.

The branch of Islam that established itself in Central Asia was Sunnism. Another teaching that made its way into the region, however, was that of the Ismailis (a major Shiite sect). In the latter half of the ninth century and in the tenth century, there were many Qarmatians in *Ma Wara al-Nahr*. (This sect was a branch of early Ismailism.) The Central Asian Qarmatians were strongly influenced by Mazdakism. One of their best-known preachers was Muhammad ibn Ahmad Nahshabi. His sermons drew a vigorous response from ordinary people. The Qarmatians were supported by many of the Samanids, which was why they had followers even among *Ma Wara al-Nahr* officials. Nahshabi advocated ideas of equality and spoke out strongly against Orthodox theologians. For this reason, he met with strong opposition from the ulama and a majority of those in power, was arrested and executed. But even after his death, the Qarmatians continued to influence various opposition forces in Central Asia for a long time.

Mainstream Ismailism, more moderate than the Qarmatians' teaching, began to spread in Central Asia in the eleventh century. It became the prevailing religion in the Pamirs and adjacent areas. There it incorporated elements of animism, including astral cults and sorcery. The religious differences between the Ismailis and the Sunni Moslems, who made up a majority of the emerging Tajik ethnic group, led to isolation of the Pamiri people and strongly influenced that people's political stance throughout history. An Ismaili community still exists in the Pamirs today.[7]

In Central Asia, the Hanafi school had the largest number of adherents. The Mutazilites, Moslem rationalists who established a separate trend in Islam from the seventh to the ninth century, had some following in Khorezm at the time of the Samanids and even somewhat later. The two centres of Sunni theology of the Hanafi school were Samarkand and Bukhara.

Islam becomes the official religion of Central Asia. Ulama and Sufi sheikhs

Central Asia began to separate itself from the Arab Caliphate at the time of the Tahirids (827–73), a local dynasty of the Baghdad Caliphate's governors.

In the Samanid state (875–999), whose capital was Bukhara and which was Central Asia's first centralised state independent of Baghdad, Islam was adopted as the official religion. Like the Tahirids, the Samanids were a Central Asian dynasty. It was founded by Saman-Khuda. (Some sources say he was a native of Balkh while other documents say he was born in an area around Samarkand or Termez.) Saman-Khuda was a close associate of al-Mamoun when al-Mamoun was the ruler of Merv. He insisted that Saman renounce Zoroastrianism and adopt Islam. In 810, Saman's grandsons helped to put down an uprising against the Arab Caliphate. Al-Mamoun appreciated these services so that when he became Caliph, he told the new governor of Khorasan to reward the Samanids' loyalty and abilities. Several members of the Samanid family were appointed governors of towns and regions, including Samarkand, Bukhara, Herat, and Shasha. They gradually expanded their possessions so that by the end of the ninth century, one of the Samanids, the ruler of Bukhara, governed a large and powerful state comprising all of Central Asia and eastern Iran.

In the tenth century, Islam occupied a prominent place in the Samanid state as its official religion. There emerged a *Ma Wara al-Nahr* school of theology, which was largely isolated from the Arab Moslem centres. *Ulama* of *Ma Wara al-Nahr* began to represent official Islam in the Samanid state and later in Central Asia's Turki states and made efforts to Islamise the nomadic population.

At the time of the Samanids, the highest religious official had the title of *ustad* ('teacher'). Later it was ousted by another title – *Sheikh ul Islam*. The second in command was the *khatib*, an official who had the right to read the *khutbah* (meaning sermon in Arabic) in the cathedral mosque during worship on Fridays. Arab governors read the *khutbah* themselves. But most Central Asian rulers did not speak Arabic, so they had to appoint an official to read the *khutbah* for them, because it had to be read in Arabic. *Ulama* in larger towns were mainly well-educated persons; they were called '*ahl al-kalam*' ('men of letters') by contemporaries. They had a good knowledge of the Arabic language, the Koran, the principal precepts of the Shariah, and Iranian literature, as well as some knowledge of various sciences. These people promoted the synthesis in which local traditions were supplemented with Arab and classical Persian traditions. Later, some well-educated Turkis became *ulama*, too. They spoke the languages of peoples who adhered to the nomadic way of life. In rural areas *mullahs* were semi-literate or illiterate. In towns, *ulama* were given posts in *divans* and other government bodies. A peculiar bureaucratic culture took shape in the region, whose long-standing (Sogdian) traditions were enriched by the experience of the Arab Caliphate and the Sasanid state.

From the latter half of the eighth century onwards, many mosques and madrasas were built in Central Asia. At first they were built by Arab governors, and later, by local rulers. They saw the construction of mosques, mausoleums, madrasas, and also palaces as a major prestige-boosting factor.

Not only palaces, but also Moslem places of worship built in Central Asia, feature local artistic traditions. Islam forbids the representation of living creatures, but there are sculptures and murals of people and animals in *Ma Wara al-Nahr*. But from the tenth century onwards, the greatest achievements were made in ornamental design – an art especially encouraged by Hanafi theologians. The architecture of mosques and madrasas was greatly influenced by local traditions too. One graphic example is the mosque in Khazar (built in the ninth century), a centric-type building without a portal, with an arched-dome ceiling.

The cultural synthesis also promoted the development of literature and science. In the years following the Arab conquest of Central Asia, the introduction of Islam was accompanied by efforts to impose the Arabic language on the region. Arabic was used in works on theology and law, in literature and science. The Sogdian tradition was discontinued, and its written language ceased to exist.

The situation began to change in the tenth century, when eastern regions seceded from the Abbasid Caliphate and Central Asia was ruled by the Tahirids, and then by the Samanids. The people of Central Asia who did not speak Arabic began to be called Tajik, and Arabic was gradually ousted by Tajiki. Only theology continued to be dominated by the Arabic language.

Freethinkers

Although Islam was adopted as the official religion of the Samanid state, this did not mean that theology came to dominate all cultural development or that culture developed in religion-related forms only. On the contrary, the ideas of freethinkers, aimed against restrictions imposed by orthodox Islam, became widely popular in Central Asia. This can be illustrated by the cultural development of *Ma Wara al-Nahr* in the ninth and tenth centuries. The best-known figures of the period who contributed a lot to that development are the physician, philosopher, and poet Abu Ali ibn-Sina (Avicenna), poets Rudaki and Firdousi (who completed a real masterpiece, the poem *Shah-nameh*, by the end of his life); and there were many other great thinkers. The library of Bukhara was famous throughout the east, the only other such library being in Shiraz.

Islamic officials varied in their attitudes to freethinking. The most enlightened upheld everything talented and original in any field of society's life. Others believed that freethinking was aimed against Islamic scholasticism, and even against Islam, and did all they could to suppress it.

The Samanid's chief rival in the struggle for Central Asia was a Turki dynasty known as the Karakhanids (972–1212), who ruled Eastern Turkestan, Jetysu (Semirechye), and the area south of the Tien Shan mountains.

At the start of the Turkis' westward advancement, *Ma Wara al-Nahr ulama* and sheikhs were active against the infidels, issuing numerous *fatwas* calling on the local population to rebuff the invaders. But as the Turkis conquered more of Central Asia, establishing states headed by Turki dynasties, the *ulama* changed their attitudes. They put greater emphasis on efforts to Islamise the nomads and popularise Islamic values among the neophytes.

In the late tenth and early eleventh centuries, the governors of the Samanid state were engaged in an increasingly intensive power struggle, while the Karakhanid state grew strong. Moslem *ulama* acted less often in support of the Samanids: one reason was that many of the

Turki rulers were members of previously Islamized clans or had adopted Islam when they came to Central Asia. The *ulama* of Bukhara denied support to the Samanids when the town was captured by Nasr, a Karakhanid ruler, in the year 999. An account by a merchant who witnessed the events says that the imams of cathedral mosques close to the Shah's court called on the people to defend the Samanids as Nasr approached Bukhara. But the people consulted *faqihs* who reportedly said this, 'If the Khanids [the Turkis] argued [with the Samanids] over religious affairs, you would be obliged to fight against them. But since they are fighting over worldly possessions, Moslems must not kill themselves or let themselves be killed.'[8]

Islam was an important catalyst promoting a synthesis of the cultures of settled Iranians and nomadic Turkis. That synthesis had begun much earlier but was most intensive in the tenth and eleventh centuries. Some scholars refuse – correctly, perhaps – to contrast *Ma Wara al-Nahr*, formerly Sogdiana, where people led a settled way of life with Jetsyu, a region populated by Turki nomads. But even after Islam was adopted, there remained major differences between the Moslem cultures of Central Asia's nomadic and settled peoples – differences which remain to this day.

Figure 1. Mausoleum Ismail Samani (IX–X c.), Bukhara

Nomadic Oghuz (Turkis) began to be converted to Islam in the eighth and ninth centuries, and the number of Moslem Oghuz rapidly increased in the tenth century. Uzbek folk tales mention Oghuz among the ancestors of the modern Uzbek people. In the late tenth century, a part of the Oghuz people began to be called Turkomans (Turkmens).

After the Samanids were defeated by the Karakhanids, the centralised state of *Ma Wara al-Nahr* collapsed, and no one made any effort to restore it for a long time. In the eleventh and twelfth centuries, Central Asia was ruled by the Karakhanids, who divided the region into the principalities, which were ruled by Ilek-khans (Karakhanid princes). As Khorezm grew strong in the early thirteenth century, the Khorezm Shah strove to build a new large state in Central Asia, but his efforts were unsuccessful. Even in that period of feudal fragmentation, Islam continued to establish itself as the pre-eminent religion of both settled and nomadic peoples and was an important statehood consolidation factor.

First Moslem missionaries

The first Moslem missionaries who worked to Islamise nomads were Sufi sheikhs (*ishans*) and dervishes. From the twelfth to the fifteenth century, an especially important role was played by a dervish *tariqa* (brotherhood) called Yasaviyah. It was founded by Ahmed Yesewi of Yasa (a Central Asian town known from the tenth century and later renamed Turkestan), who was traditionally considered the forefather of all Turki Sufis. Ahmed Yesewi (who died in 1166) was a disciple of a Turki sheikh, then moved to Bukhara and became a follower of Yusuf al-Hamadani, a native of Hamadan province in the Baghdad Caliphate, who spent most of his life preaching his 'salvation' theory in Central Asia. Many famous Sufis of Central Asia were descendants of Yusuf al-Hamadani.

Ahmed Yesewi developed a teaching that combined Iranian and Turki Sufis' traditions, thereby mixing the cultures of settled farmers and nomads in practice. That teaching played a major role in Islamising nomadic Turki tribes. Verses composed by Ahmed himself and his followers – wandering dervishes – promoted interaction between Iranian and Turkic languages. Being a *tariqa* of wandering dervishes, Yasaviyah had no branches or permanent settlements, except those established near sheikhs' tombs. Wandering dervishes spread Islam throughout Turkestan and also among Kirghiz and Kazakh nomads. In the thirteenth and fourteenth centuries, Yesewi was known as Khazrat-i Turkestan.

Yasaviyah was a spiritual ancestor of Bahaaddin Naqshbandi, the leader of another Sufi brotherhood that played a prominent role in Central Asia. At first, the Naqshbandiyah brotherhood was urban and Iranian, but later it absorbed many traditions of Turki nomads and contributed to their Islamisation, promoting a synthesis of Iranian and Turki, farmers' and nomads' cultures.

Bahaaddin Naqshbandi (1318–89) was not the founder of the *tariqa* that bore his name. The *tariqa* dates back to al-Hamadani (who died in 1140). Al-Hamadani's disciple, Abdul-Khaliq al-Ghudjduwani (who died in 1220), was considered the founder of a new 'path' in mystical life, free from ostentatious, distracting rites and conforming to the principle that 'the outward life is for the world and the inner life is for God'. According to J. S. Trimingham, who wrote one of the most comprehensive works about Sufi orders, that 'path' has stood the test of time, retaining the hallmark of Abdul Khaliq's genius in all that has to do with mentorship, teaching, and ritual purity.[9] That path was followed by Bahaaddin. Like most people after whom *tariqa* were named, Bahaaddin had no organisation when he took over as the *tariqa*'s leader. He gathered a few followers and taught Abdul Khaliq's *tariqa* to them.

Muhammad Bahaaddin was a Tajik, born in a village near Bukhara. He was taught by two Bukhara mentors, but he knew many Tajik, too. J. S. Trimingham relates a romantic story about Bahaaddin's encounter with dervish Khalil, who later became sultan. Bahaaddin served Sultan Khalil for six years, but, following Khalil's fall, lost interest in his secular career. He came back to his native village near Bukhara and resumed his religious activities. In terms of promoting the spread of Islam in Central Asia, Bahaaddin did much to strengthen Turkis' links with the Sunna. Bahaaddin's mausoleum with the nearby monastery (a splendid building constructed in 1544) was one of Central Asia's most visited holy places.

Another major brotherhood was Qadiriyah. Naqshbandiyah and Qadiriyah were Sunni brotherhoods. Qubraviyah, which also had a considerable following in Central Asia, is usually considered to belong to the Shi'a tradition. It was founded by Nadjm al-Din al-Qubra (1145–1221), a native of Khiva (Khorezm). After a course of ascesis taken under the guidance of prominent Sufis in Egypt, al-Qubra came back to Khorezm, built a *khanaqah*, and educated Sufis there. But none of his followers founded new brotherhoods. He wrote a manual for neophytes – *Sifat al-adat* ('Rules of Conduct') – in Persian, which made him famous, and contributed to the Iranisation of Sufism. Al-Qubra's followers worked hard to Islamise nomads, including the leaders of Mongol tribes that conquered Central Asia in the thirteenth century.

The Mongol conquest

The Mongol conquest, causing an unprecedented destruction of Central Asia's greatest cultural centres, laid in ruins many Moslem cultural monuments. It was a great upheaval. The shock it produced is best illustrated by what ibn al-Asir wrote about the invasion: 'If someone said that nothing like this has been done in the world ever since Allah Almighty and Supreme created man, he would be right.'[10] In Bukhara, most mosques, *madrasas*, and markets lay in ruins. Samarkand, Khorezm, and other major towns of Central Asia were greatly ravaged too. Most *ulama* supported local rulers who fought hard against the invaders. Sheikh Nadjm al-Din al-Qubra died a hero's death defending Khorezm.

But Central Asian states failed to unite against the Mongols. The most significant popular uprising against the Mongol invaders was staged in Bukhara in 1238. It was led by Mahmud Tarabi. Many sheikhs and *ulama* supported the uprising and even declared Tarabi caliph, the leader of faithful Moslems, emphasising the fact that the Bukharans were fighting under the banner of Islam. But some theologians and noblemen supported the Mongols and helped them to suppress the rebellion.

However, that uprising was a serious warning to the Mongol tribal leaders who were then ruling Central Asia. The Mongols began making efforts to encourage Moslem sheikhs and *ulama*, as well as Moslem merchants, to help them to establish peace after the devastating wars.

A large part of Central Asia, the territory between the Amalyk River and the Amu Darya, was granted to Chagatai, the second son of the famous Mongol conqueror Genghis Khan (1155–1227). Chagatai was an advocate of Mongol law and an enemy of Islam. But he did have a Moslem adviser. In the 1260s, a khan of Chagatai's state, Mubarek-Shah, and Borak-Khan adopted Islam. Mubarek-Shah was the first khan to be enthroned in *Ma Wara al-Nahr*, rather than in the Ili River area. Mubarek-Shah brought along Mongol nomadic clans. They also adopted Islam, which accelerated their Turkisation.

Borak-Khan, the ruler of the Golden Horde, which comprised the northern part of Central Asia (Khorezm) in the middle of the thirteenth century, also adopted Islam. He decided to make a public declaration of loyalty to Islam to a Sufi sheikh, rather than to a Sunni *alim* (sing. of *ulama*). He went to Bukhara and adopted Islam in the presence of Sufis of Qubraviyah.

Other descendants of Genghis Khan and their governors began to adopt Islam, and trading rights were often granted to Moslem merchants in preference to others. In many towns, local dynasties.

remained, and Moslem *ulama* and sheikhs retained their positions.

In the middle of the thirteenth century, Bukhara was delegated to a merchant named Masudibeg who built beautiful mosques and a *madrasa* known as the Masudiye Madrasa there. But Masudibeg's rule did not last long. In 1273, under the first rulers from among Genghis Khan's descendants, the Khulaguids (1256 to the middle of the fourteenth century), Bukhara was again devastated by the Mongols. Masudibeg's *madrasa* was burned down, along with great numbers of handwritten books. The town was ravaged, and its entire population forced to flee. Bukhara stood almost empty for seven years and ceased to play a role as a centre of trade, crafts, or culture for a long time afterwards.

From about 1219, when Genghis Khan invaded eastern Turkestan and Jetysu, to the end of the thirteenth century, Central Asia was governed by non-Moslem rulers, and Islam was not the official religion. But during the reign of the Khulaguids, the situation began to change. A Khulaguid ruler Ghazan Khan (1295–1304) adopted Sunni Islam. His example was followed by Mongol warriors, military leaders, and courtiers. Pagan temples built under previous Mongol rulers were destroyed. On Ghazan Khan's orders, magnificent new mosques were built in Tabriz, the capital of the Khulaguid state.

Islam's status as the official religion of Central Asia began to be restored some time later, during the reign of Kebek Khan (1318–26), who strove to establish strong links with Islamic cultural centres of *Ma Wara al-Nahr*. But the position of Islam was not the same as under previous rulers, in that the Islamic cause was promoted mainly by Sufi sheikhs rather than by *ulama*. Tombs became new symbols of Islam, just like mosques. A tomb, a dervish monastery, and a *zikr* circle (a *zikr* being a rite of gratification and praise of Allah, with an accompanying psychological ritual) were outward expressions of a living popular religion, appealing to both Iranians and Turkis.

Sufis played a major role in the Islamisation of Central Asia. They materialised the trend towards religious syncretism, which had been typical of religious development in pre-Islamic Central Asia, and worked to adapt Islam to local religious traditions – not so much with the aid of their mysticism, but through veneration of saints and their tombs, which had been an inalienable part of Sufism from the very outset. Any description of Central Asia would be incomplete without the image of a wandering dervish – a figure that played a prominent role in the life of Central Asia and all its people, poverty-stricken peasants and noblemen alike.

Sufis Islamised the holy places that existed in pre-Islamic Central Asia – Buddhist stupas, Zoroastrian sanctuaries, and even some Christian churches – and turned them over to sheikhs. Legends about pre-Islamic saints and their graves were incorporated into the Sufi tradition. Tombs were guarded by dervishes, who lived in *khanaqahs*, where pilgrims were received. Sufi sheikhs were closer to ordinary people than *ulama* – representatives of Islamic authorities – and dervishes were not very different in status from the lower strata of society. But some *ulama* had close links with sheikhs and even acted as sheikhs. Clergymen regained their official status in the state system, and some actually became government officials. In Termez, all power belonged to hereditary sayyids, known as *khudavand-zadehs*, who were especially influential in the 1330s–60s.

So a prominent Russian orientalist, W. Barthold (1869–1930), had every reason to conclude that the domination of Islam and its culture had become complete in Central Asia by the time of Genghis Khan's successors (in the early fourteenth century).[11]

The political situation in Central Asian territories remained extremely unstable throughout the period of Mongol rule. In the middle of the thirteenth century, the Golden Horde laid claims to Central Asia. The Chagatai khans and the Khulaguids were divided, too. Struggles never ceased between those who advocated the development of permanent-population areas and the cultural centres of *Ma Wara al-Nahr* and the Mongol military and tribal leaders who favoured nomadic traditions. All this led finally to the elimination of Mongol control over Central Asia and the establishment to Timur (Tamerlane, 1336–1405) as the supreme ruler of the entire region.

Islam and Central Asia's culture under Timur and the Tumurids

Timur is very popular in Central Asia. There is a magnificent monument symbolising his grandeur in the middle of the steppes between Tashkent and Samarkand. His reign promoted the consolidation of Islam in Central Asia, and Islam, in turn, was the basis on which Timur's state was consolidated.

Timur was born in a village called Khodfa Ilgar, not far from Shahrisiabz. His father, Taraghai, was a Barlas beg, who, although not very rich, was quite influential. Stories about Timur's youth are found in works by ibn-Arabshah and Spanish diplomat Ruy Gonzalez de Clavijo and in Russian chronicles. Clavijo writes, for instance, that after successful raids into neighbouring territories young Timur always: 'feasted with his warriors; partly because of this and partly because he was brave and kind and generous in sharing what he had, people were attracted to him, so finally he had 300 horsemen in his unit'.[12] Timur displayed leadership rather early in his life and became very popular with Barlas people, especially with young nomad warriors.

Timur spoke Turki and Tajiki and knew the life of both nomadic stockbreeders and settled people, rural and urban. He often visited Shahrisiabz, whose ruler was his grandfather, *hajji* Barlas.

Shahrisiabz was a Moslem town, and Moslem sheikhs were held in great respect there. Timur had a deep respect for Sheikh ad-Din Qulal, his father's confessor. He said that many of his achievements were a result of Qulal's prayers.

At the end of the fourteenth century, Timur established his rule over the whole of *Ma Wara al-Nahr*. Even before he captured Balkh, a sheikh named Bereke presented a drum and a banner (the symbols of authority) to him. The sheikh, a native of Mecca, later became Timur's chief confessor. According to his chronicles, Bereke predicted a great future for Timur. Following the capture of Balkh, Timur was proclaimed the supreme ruler of *Ma Wara al-Nahr* by his military commanders. He had the support of Moslem sheikhs and *ulama*, too. Two brothers, Abu-l Iaali and Ali Akbar, well-known sheikhs of Termez who bore the title of *khudavand-zadeh*, came to Balkh to serve Timur. Their service consolidated Timur's alliance with the theologians of *Ma Wara al-Nahr*, an alliance which remained strong throughout his long reign.

Timur was always an Islamic ruler, holding high the green banner of Islam. He showed genuine interest in establishing Islam among nomadic peoples, and therefore in supporting not only *ulama* but also the first Islamic missionaries – dervishes and sheikhs (*ishans*), so he always treated these peoples with respect. On his orders, a magnificent mausoleum was built in honour of *hajji* Ahmed Yesewi in Yasa at the end of the fourteenth century.

During the reign of Timur's successors, Sheikh al-Ahrar of the Naqshbandiyah brotherhood played an important role as a mediator among three Timurid sultans.

In 1370, Timur moved to Samarkand where he built strong walls, a citadel, and a palace. After subjugating Khorezm, Timur ruled all of Central Asia except Jetysu and the lower reaches of the Syr Darya. The rest of Central Asia was added to his possessions in a war against the Golden Horde. In 1391, Timur moved into what is now Kazakhstan, On his orders, words were carved on a piece of rock near Ulutag Mountain saying that he had led 200,000 warriors 'to defeat Tikhtamysh Khan'. That piece of rock, found in the Karsakpai mines in the mid-1930s, is now at the Hermitage museum in St Petersburg. Timur's victory over the Golden Horde and the destruction of Saray put an end to Mongol rule of Central Asia and Russia.

It is a well-known fact that the Russian army's victory on Kulikovo plain was the Mongols' first overwhelming defeat. It broke the backbone of the once-powerful state, and Timur became ruler of all

Central Asia. His subsequent campaigns in the Transcaucasus, Iran, India, and China did not really contribute to the consolidation of the Central Asian state: they were aimed at conquering better territories and seizing booty. Indirectly, however, these campaigns strengthened Timur's state. Timur was well aware that European and West Asian trade with the Far East offered major advantages to Central Asian towns. He aimed to disrupt the northern trade route, across the Golden Horde, and to bring the trade traffic back on to the old route across Central Asia. Only Timur's death and the resulting political complications prevented the complete realisation of that plan.

As the ruler of a multilingual empire, Timur always made special efforts to consolidate the unity and integrity of its core. His Central Asian and Iranian possessions were united in a single state. Timur did not divide *Ma Wara al-Nahr* or grant any part of it (except Fergana) to any other ruler. Islam was the most important factor in his policies. His confessor, sheikh Bereke, 'substantiated with prayers what Timur did with his sword'. Timur was pleased that Bereke prayed for victory before major battles.

Timur was well aware of Islam's importance for the consolidation of his territorial possessions. He wrote in his Code: 'I worked hard to spread the religion of Allah and the law of Muhammad, the vessel chosen by God, I supported Islam at all times and in all places. I founded my power on Islam . . . The restoration of the religion and divine law consolidated my power.'[13]

Timur leaned mainly on Sunni Islam. In Shiite Khorasan, he restored Sunnism. In Mazandaran, he punished Shiite dervishes but he was prepared to uphold Shiites when it suited his political interests. In Syria, he spoke in defence of Ali and his descendants, which earned him the image of a zealous Shiite.

Under Timur, *Ma Wara al-Nahr* became a major Moslem centre. In Samarkand, the capital of Timur's state, magnificent monuments of Moslem culture were created, and their artistic value has not diminished with time. Clavijo was amazed by Timur's building zeal and by the scale of his projects. Timur worked to make Samarkand larger and more beautiful than any capital before it. He built many new palaces and mosques and renovated the whole town, opening specially equipped market-places, craftsmen's areas, etc. Some of the buildings are still in existence today: a remarkable mausoleum in the **Shah-i Zinda** ensemble; the burial place of the Moslem saint Qusam Abbas; Timur's cathedral mosque, now known as the **Bibi-Khanom** Mosque and the **Gur-e Amir** Mausoleum, where Timur, his sons, and his grandsons are buried. During Timur's reign, many beautiful mosques were built in other areas of *Ma Wara al-Nahr*, too: one of the best-known is the Khodja Ahmad Mosque in Turkestan.

Figure 2. Mausoleum Gur-e Amir (XIV c.), Samarkand

Figure 3. Shah-i Zinda ensemble (XIV c.), Samarkand

Figure 4. Bibi-Khanom Mosque (XIV c.), Samarkand

Cultural achievement under Ulugh beg

Vivid new pages were added to the history of Moslem culture in Central Asia when Samarkand was ruled by Timur's grandson, Ulugh beg Muhammad Taragaiya (1394–1449). Unlike his grandfather, Ulugh beg had no talent for war or statesmanship. He is known in Central Asian history as the creator of many cultural monuments and as a man who protected freethinking, inspired and organised scientific research and cultural development in Samarkand, and wrote scientific works of inestimable value.

From the time of Timur, Samarkand's cultural life was marked by freethinking. Timur detested ostentatious piety and did not allow orthodox *ulama* to interfere with the life and work of poets, artists, architects, and scientists or even to insist that women spend every minute of their lives in the women's sections of their homes. He strove hard to establish schools for theology as well as secular science and was supported in his efforts by the better-educated *ulama*. In Central Asia and in other parts of the Moslem world, these people always believed that true Islam, far from denying the need for science, actually required scientific development and knowledge. Traditions laid down by Timur were preserved and pursued by Ulugh beg. It was an especially important factor that Ulugh beg's work was supported by Isam ad-Din, Sheikh ul-Islam of Samarkand. A well-educated and clever man, he was a descendant of the author of *Khidaya* – a famous work on theology and law.

New *madrasas* were built in Samarkand and Bukhara on Ulugh beg's orders. There was nothing special about that: all rulers built *madrasas*. But Ulugh beg assigned a special role to the schools. The following words were carved above the main portal of the Bukhara *madrasa*: 'Learning is an obligation of every Moslem man and woman'. This certainly referred to learning theology. But the reference to women was new and significant and in this context it should be pointed out that Ulugh beg and his followers had progressive views concerning the position of women in Islamic society. Some scholars believe that the phrase carved on the Bukhara *madrasa* refers to secular learning, too, but that is only a guess. It is significant, however, that the words were carved in Bukhara – the stronghold of the most conservative sheikhs and theologians.

In Samarkand, Ulugh beg personally supervised the construction of a *madrasa*. The building is still there today, but it has suffered badly from the ravages of time and the indifference of later generations. The **Ulugh beg madrasa** stands on Registan Square. Just across from it, a *khanaqah* (a hostel for wandering Sufi dervishes), famous for its magnificent dome, was built later. According to Babur, who visited

Figure 5. Madrasa Ulugh beg (XV c.), Samarkand

Samarkand in the early sixteenth century, this dome was the largest in the world. But the *khanaqah* was destroyed by the seventeenth century, and the Shindar Mosque built in its place. Ulugh beg built the entrance portal of the famous necropolis, the **Shah-i Zinda**. The tympanums of the main portal of Ulugh beg's *madrasa* in Samarkand represent the starry sky. This means that, in addition to theology, people studied secular sciences there, especially astronomy which was taught by Kadi-zade Rumi, 'the Plato of his time'.

One of his students was a young poet, Nur od-Din Abd or-Rahman ibn Ahmad Jami. W. Barthold quotes medieval historians relating an interesting story about the appointment of the *madrasa*'s *mudarris*. Shortly before the *madrasa* was inaugurated, Ulugh beg was asked who would be its *mudarris*. He said he wanted to find a man well versed in all sciences. A man named Maulana Muhammad Khorezmi heard this and said he qualified for the job. But his dirty appearance and shabby clothes rendered his words unconvincing. However, Ulugh beg tested the man's knowledge and was satisfied. Maulana Muhammad was washed thoroughly and dressed in fine clothes. On the day the *madrasa* was inaugurated, he delivered his first lecture as its *mudarris* to an audience of 90 scholars, but only Kadi-zade Rumi and Ulugh beg understood what he was talking about. At the same time, the famous Ulugh beg observatory was built; Ulugh beg's contemporaries said it was then the best observatory in the world. Ulugh beg worked there for many years, producing fascinating astronomical charts.

The better-educated *ulama* not only supported Ulugh beg in his scientific endeavours, but even took part in secular entertainments, although they were censured by orthodox *ulama*. For example, the Sheikh ul Islam invited female singers to a feast organised to celebrate the completion of new bathhouses – and was criticised by the *muhtasib*.

Many *ulama* of Samarkand protested against the behaviour of their learned ruler and the Sheikh ul-Islam's support for him. Opposition was especially strong from the conservative sheikhs and *ulama* of Bukhara. Among Ulugh beg's opponents were influential sheikhs: Muhammad Parsa in Bukhara, Hasan Attar in Samarkand, and Yakoub Charkhi in Badakhshan. Sheikh Charkhi was the preceptor of Ubaidallah Khoja Ahrar, Central Asia's most conservative dervish, who acted to suppress all freethinking in the latter half of the fifteenth century.

Conservative sheikhs and *ulama* supported Ulugh beg's son Abdul Latif, who acted against his father to seize the Timurid throne. Abdul Latif organised the assassination of Ulugh beg who was killed in 1449, when he and *hajji* Muhammad Khosrow left Samarkand to make a *hajj* to Makkah. Only a year later, the patricidal ruler was killed by Ulugh beg's followers, supported by the people. The situation became very unstable, with power shifting from one ruler to another. The Timurids were split into opposing groups, as were Sufi sheikhs and theologians who held official government posts.

In the latter half of the fifteenth century, the main centre of Central Asian cultural development was Herat. Samarkand, Bukhara, Tashkent, Fergana, and other major principalities were governed by rulers who waged wars against each other. Amidst this turmoil, Central Asia became divided between Safavid Iran and the state of Shaibani Khan, who leaned on Uzbek nomads.

Islam in the Central Asian khanates (in the fourteenth and the first half of the fifteenth century). The differences in Islam as practised by settled populations and nomads

An Uzbek state began to emerge in Central Asia as Uzbek nomads advanced into Central Asian steppes, conquering major towns of *Ma Wara al-Nahr*. The Uzbek state was founded by Shaibani Khan, grandson of the most powerful of the last Genhisids, Abulkhair. In the 1440s, Abulkhair conquered some territories ruled by the Timurids in the lower reaches of the Syr Darya and temporarily united Uzbek, Mangit, and other tribes of Deshti Kipchak into a single nomad state.

Abulkhair brought up his two grandsons – Shaibani and his brother – because their parents had died when they were small boys. He did his best to give them a good Moslem education. When they were young, the boys were patronised by the Timurid governor of Turkestan, who hoped that in future they would keep Uzbek tribes from raiding his towns. Shaibani lived in Bukhara for a while, completing a classical education under the guidance of Muhammad Hitaiya, one of the best reciters of the Koran. Throughout his life, Shaibani preserved his love of theology, science, and poetry. In his development, he was greatly influenced by Sufis. Shaibani was a *murid* of Sheikh Jamaladdin Aziz. But after Aziz refused to support his daring plan to subjugate the Timurids' possessions in Central Asia, Shaibani became a disciple of Sheikh Mansur of Bukhara. Mansur understood at once that 'the Uzbek wants to be padishah', but he upheld his bold schemes. After lunch one day, as a servant took away the dishes and was folding the tablecloth starting with the edges, the Sheikh reportedly said to Shaibani: 'When you fold a tablecloth, you start with the edges; when you conquer a state, start with the edges.'[14] That conversation, described by Sufi sources, shows that Sheikh Mansur approved of Shaibani's plan to conquer *Ma Wara al-Nahr* and unite Uzbek territories into a single state. A major role in that plan was reserved for Islam.

As Shaibani began to conquer *Ma Wara al-Nahr*, the sheikhs and *ulama* were divided in their response. Some dervishes and sheikhs were against Shaibani, others, like Sheikh Mansur of Bukhara, supported him from the very start. Even the great Khoja of Samarkand, Muhammad Yahya, who had been loyal to the Timurids and fought to defend Samarkand, cooperated with Shaibani after the town was captured. Soon after Samarkand was captured, a plot to provoke an uprising was exposed. Uzbek emirs accused Muhammad Yahya of hostile actions and demanded that he be put to death, like other mutinous noblemen of Samarkand. But Shaibani refused to punish Yahya and sent him to Makkah instead. On his way there, however, Muhammad Yahya was killed by Uzbek nomads, who acted, legend says, against Shaibani's orders.

For a long time, Moslem *ulama* encountered considerable difficulties in consolidating their influence over Uzbek nomads, but they finally succeeded. In the early sixteenth century, Shaibani Khan subjugated a considerable part of Central Asia. During the conquest of *Ma Wara al-Nahr*, many Uzbek tribes of Shaibani's ulus, as well as some Kazakh tribes, shifted to a settled way of life, but many other Uzbek and Kazakh people remained itinerant within the same territories. Shaibani's state united nomads with the settled population of the Timurids' Central Asian territories. But his state was weak: it was weakened by conflicts between nomads and settled farmers and by rivalry among khans, nomadic uluses, and rulers of big towns and farming communities developing around them. Shaibani's state was demolished by Iran, toward which much of Central Asia traditionally gravitated. At that time, Iran was ruled by the Safavids, a Shiite dynasty of Iranian–Azeri origin. The founder of this dynasty, Ismail I, came from a family of Shiite sheikhs of Ardabil, which was held in great respect by the Turki tribes of Azerbaijan. He defeated Shaibani Khan totally at Merv in a battle in which Shaibani was killed. Shah Ismail had Shaibani's skull mounted in gold and used it as a cup. The skin of Shaibani's head was stuffed with straw and sent to Sultan Bayazid II of Turkey, the head of orthodox Sunnism, as a symbol of the Shiites' triumph over the Sunnis.

Safavid–Shaibanid conflict

Throughout the sixteenth century, conflict was continuous between Safavid Iran and the Uzbek state headed by the Shaibanids. Even after their crushing defeat, the Uzbeks retained control over a large part of *Ma Wara al-Nahr*. Babur failed to consolidate his rule in Central Asia, even though he captured Samarkand in 1512. In Samarkand, he read *khutab* in the cathedral mosque acknowledging the sovereignty of Shah Ismail and began to mint coins bearing the names of Shiite *imams*. The people of Samarkand and other territories in Cental Asia were outraged by the official recognition of Shiism. Sunni *ulama* and sheikhs (*ishans*) supported Uzbek sultans who fought and defeated Babur and then the army of Iran that intervened to support him. In 1513, Samarkand was regained by Uzbek rulers, this time forever. Babur decided to end his campaigns for Central Asia. In 1525, he moved his army into India, where he founded the Mogul Empire.

In Central Asia, wars continued between the Safavids and the Shaibanid state. Territorial claims were substantiated by arguments that Sunnism or Shiism should be the official religion of this or that territory. These arguments are found in letters written by the rulers and *ulama* of *Ma Wara al-Nahr* in the sixteenth century to *ulama* of Meshed, criticising the religious policies of the Safavid rulers.[15] For centuries, *Ma Wara al-Nahr* and Iran had been united in a single state, and educated people of the period (both Islamic and secular scholars) maintained that the official religion of that state should be Sunnism. So the rulers and *ulama* of *Ma Wara al-Nahr* protested not only against the penetration of Shiism into Central Asia, but also against its consolidation in Iran proper. They invited support from the theologians and rulers of other states, such as the Baghdad Caliphate and even India. The theologians of Baghdad supported their colleagues in *Ma Wara al-Nahr*. But Emperor Akbar of India, a great descendant of Babur, refused to support them. He rejected the proposal of the Uzbek ruler Abdallah Khan (1583–98) for the formation of an alliance against the Shiite Safavids, to make it possible for Sunni pilgrims to pass through Iran to Makkah. But Uzbek khans took advantage of hostile relations between Shiite Iran and the Sunni Ottoman Empire. The wars waged by Ottoman sultans against the Safavids kept Iran too busy to attend to *Ma Wara al-Nahr*. Taking advantage of this, Uzbek khans made regular raids on Shiite Khorasan and strove to consolidate their own state in Central Asia. After Shaibani Khan's death, the most important periods in the history of the Shaibanids when Islam was especially effective as an integrating factor were the reigns of Ubaydallah Khan (1533–9) and Abdallah Khan (1583–98).

Ubaydallah Khan was educated in the Sufi spirit. He was named after Ubaydallah khoja Ahrar, Central Asia's famous fifteenth-century sheikh. Ubaydallah was a disciple of Sheikh Makhdoumi Azam and had many of his teacher's treatises in his library. He was well educated: he spoke Turki, Persian, and Arabic, and wrote poems. But he was also a tough warrior who did much to reunite his country and to spread Islam among nomads.

Abdallah Khan made the last attempt to unite all of Central Asia into a strong centralised state. He considerably expanded the international relations of the Uzbek state, consolidating the alliance with the Ottoman Empire and establishing stable trade and political relations with the Russian state (the Moscow state), whose territory had then been expanded by Ivan the Terrible to reach Deshti Kipchak. But the Shaibanids' efforts to establish control over Kirghiz and Kazakh nomadic tribes, which had never been ruled by *Ma Wara al-Nahr* sovereigns, aggravated relations with the Kazakh Khanate. In 1554, the Kazakh Khan Tevkkel proposed to Czar Fyodor of Moscow that they should join forces to fight against Abdallah Khan, and even declared himself a vassal of the Moscow state. But Tevkkel was defeated by Abdallah Khan, and his successor concluded peace with the Uzbeks, retaining Turkestan with Tashkent for the Kazakh Khanate.

Like all the Shaibanids, Abdallah Khan pursued a policy in which Islam played a major role. He gave much attention to the construction of *madrasas, mosques,* and *khanaqahs.* Moslem imams, and especially Sufi sheikhs (*ishans*), had a prominent position in the Shaibanid state.

Figure 6. Madrasa Kutlug Murad Inoi, Khiva

They retained their *waqfs* and were given new ones. In Shahrukh, for instance, Abdallah Khan built a mosque for ishan Shah Emir Asadullah and gave him a *waqf* – a large area of land with villages – exempted indefinitely from taxation. Uzbek khans enlisted the support of Sufi orders (brotherhoods) and actively involved them in political rivalry. Sheikhs not only supported their rulers but even supplied dervishes of unquestioning loyalty to commit assassinations for them. Some of the major adversaries of the Shaibanids – Emir Ibrahim of Tashkent, Burkhan Sultan of Bukhara and many others were stabbed by *murids* acting on their sheikhs' orders. The situation was further aggravated by the struggle between the Shiite Order of Qubraviyah and the Sunni Order of Naqshbandiyah, at that time the two most influential brotherhoods. But on the whole, Islam was a factor promoting unification rather than disintegration in the period when Central Asian states and ethnic groups were established.

The period of the Shaibanids was a time of intensive development of the Uzbek ethnic group. During this period, the Uzbek language absorbed many Persian–Tajiki and Old Turki elements. But for a long time, the Persian literary language was used in the official documents and literary works of the Uzbek khanates. However, as Shiism was established in Iran, the culture of Central Asia gradually separated itself from Iranian culture.

Khiva, Bukhara, and Kokand Khanates

From the seventeenth century to the first half of the nineteenth century, Central Asia, or parts of it, were incorporated into several states whose official religion was Sunnism. At the time of incorporation into the Russian Empire, the largest of these states were the Khiva, Bukhara, and Kokand Khanates.

The Khiva Khanate was established in the territory of Khorezm after the latter seceded permanently from the Shaibanid state. Khorezm was established as a separate state earlier than other territories because of its geographic location. The Khorezm oasis had always been isolated from Central Asia's centres, Samarkand and Bukhara, by arid steppes. Trade routes that had existed since ancient times directed Khorezm's interests towards the Volga River region and the Trans-Caspian countries. The factor that made it difficult for neighbouring states to conquer Khorezm was the existence of the warlike Turkoman tribes roaming the area around it. After the Amu Darya changed its course in the latter half of the sixteenth century, flowing into the Aral Sea instead of the Caspian, the area around Urgench (Khorezm) turned to desert. Many of its people moved southeastwards, to the vicinity of Khiva, which became the capital of a new khanate. Ethnically, this khanate's population was extremely diverse, comprising settled Turkised local people, Turkoman nomads, and semi-nomadic ethnic groups. The khan's authority spread mainly over towns and adjacent areas populated by settled farmers. In these places Islam became the official religion.

The Bukhara Khanate was founded in the territory that had been the core of the Shaibanid state. (The Shaibanids had vanished from the historical scene by the end of the sixteenth century.) In the seventeenth and eighteenth centuries, Bukhara still elected its khan – a tradition inherited from the time of the nomadic Uzbek. When a new ruler was elected, he was lifted on a sheet of white felt. The ceremony was attended by the khan's close relatives, tribal emirs, and Sufi sheikhs (*ishans*). Another custom was also preserved for a long time: a newly elected khan had to sit on a sacred 'grey stone' in Samarkand. Traditionally, it was the khan's prerogative to mint coins and to have *khutaba* acknowledging his sovereignty read in the cathedral mosque on Fridays. The khan was the supreme secular and religious leader. *Ulama* held important government posts and had a monopoly on education and jurisprudence.

Islam was the official ideology of all the khanates of Central Asia, but in Bukhara the system of official Islamic authority and the state structure were interlinked more closely than elsewhere. All war crimes and civil cases were tried by Moslem judges (*qadis*) in accordance with

Shariah precepts; the judges were headed by a supreme judge (the *Qadi Kolon*). The highest religious official was the Sheikh ul-Islam, the highest authority for any appeals against judicial decisions. Legal advice was provided by *muftis*, who were selected from the *ulama*.

Government posts were held mainly by *ulama* who were also *saadah* – those who were traditionally considered to be direct descendants of Muhammad. Only *ulama* had the right to appear without a belt in the presence of the khan.

In Bukhara, as well as in other Central Asian territories and in the Moslem east in general, there were two types of schools: *maktabs* (lower-level education) and *madrasas* (higher institutions of learning). In *maktabs*, the children were taught to read and write and educated in the spirit of Moslem piety. In *madrasas*, people mainly studied the Shariah, Moslem theology, and philosophy. They also studied a few subjects not related to theology: Arabic grammar, logic, rhetoric, the first four rules of arithmetic, the fundamentals of algebra and geometry. *Madrasas* existed on revenues from their *waqfs*. The rulers of Bukhara attached great importance to Moslem *maktabs* and *madrasas* because well-educated people were needed to fill positions in the government and at court.

Sufi sheikhs (*ishans*) and dervishes did not, as a rule, hold official posts, but their influence on political affairs and on the khans was great. Many khans were *murids* (disciples) of the most influential sheikhs. However, there was no unity within Sufi orders, and many dervishes supported people who rebelled against their khans. In Tashkent and Fergana, dervish khojas (traditionally viewed as descendants of the first three successors of Muhammad) strove to separate their possessions from Bukhara. As a ruling dynasty, the khojas did not stay in power for a long time, but their efforts led to the establishment of an independent khanate in Fergana (whose capital was Kokand), which comprised nearly the whole of the Syr Darya area and part of Jetysu. In the early eighteenth century, the Kokand Khanate was ruled by an Uzbek dynasty of the Ming tribe. Like Khiva, the Kokand Khanate was ethnically diverse, and antagonisms remained between the settled population and the nomads. The nomads were also longer in adopting Islam.

All three khanates were similar in terms of official Islamic organisation, the role of *ulama* in government structures, and the influence of *ulama* and *ishans,* but there were differences, too. The *ulama* of Bukhara and Samarkand were the most enlightened. In Khiva, many *ulama* and secular feudalists had troops of their own, and the khan often enlisted their support in the struggle against the tribal nobility.

As already mentioned, sheikhs (*ishans*) and dervishes did not belong to official Islamic authorities. But they did work to combine their teaching with Shariah dogmas. An overwhelming majority of Central Asia's Sufi orders professed Sunnism. The Nakshbandiyah Order still had the largest following. Other major orders were Qadirshiyah and Qubraviyah. (The latter had many followers in Khiva.)

By the time the Central Asian khanates were established, most sheikhs had renounced asceticism, which they had preached for a long time before. They had become rich and were active in politics. Every *ishan* had *murids* who were dervishes of his brotherhood. Dervishes roamed towns and farming communities, staying in *khanaqahs* and living on alms. *Ishans* had as well as dervishes, many *murids* representing various social strata – craftsmen, merchants, farmers, landlords, and even khans. (Examples illustrating this can be found in Bukhara, Khiva, and Kokand.)

Throughout the history of Central Asia, Sufism clearly influenced cultural development.

From the sixteenth to the eighteenth century, there was a noticeable decline in the cultural development of the Central Asian khanates, compared with the era of 'cultural synthesis' that followed the establishment of Islam as the official religion of the early Moslem states in Central Asia. However, there were philosophers and poets, including some strongly influenced by Sufism, who contributed greatly to the development of Central Asian culture. The influence of Sufism was most evident in the work of Sufi Allayar, a seventeenth-century mystic and poet. His poems were sung with other religious verses and were very popular in urban and rural areas.

In the early nineteenth century, there was a cultural revival in the old cultural centres – Bukhara and Samarkand – and also in Khiva, with a major role played not only by Sufism, but also by *madrasas* (centres of enlightenment that strove to preserve the Islamic cultural tradition).

Islam among nomads

Nomadic tribes, previously all but isolated from the cultural life of *Ma Wara al-Nahr* despite their proximity to major trade routes, had by that time acquired broader contacts with Central Asian towns and agricultural oases. In fact, Islam began to emerge as the pre-eminent religion of Central Asian nomads as late as the period from the sixteenth to the eighteenth centuries, although some tribes had adopted it much earlier.

By that time, nomadic tribes had developed into large nomadic ethnoses – the Kazakh, the Turkomans, and the Kirghiz. There were some smaller tribes in Central Asia, but their role in its history was not as important.

In contrast to the Uzbek nomads, and especially the Tajiks, who had begun to adopt a settled way of life much earlier, the Kazakh, the Turkomans, and the Kirghiz were not greatly influenced by the culture that had existed in the urban and rural communities of *Ma Wara al-Nahr* since ancient times; most of them remained nomadic stockbreeders until the Russian conquest – and many even after it. As before, the nomadic peoples' cultural centre was Yasa.

Of all the nomadic ethnic groups, the Kazakh were the only people that established a state of their own in the period between the sixteenth and the eighteenth centuries. By that time, they had small farming communities scattered along the Syr Darya and the Turgai and in Jetysu. Kazakh people began to adopt Islam as early as the tenth century, but it became their main religion only after Kazakh khanates were established. In the first half of the eighteenth century, Kazakh nomads roamed large territories between the lower Yaik and the Caspian in the north and China. The Kazakh were divided into three Zhuzes (hordes) – the Ulu, or Usun, Zhuz (the Large Horde), the Orta, or Akto Zhuz (the Middle Horde), and the Kishi, or the Alchin, Zhuz (the Small Horde). The Ulu Zhuz became dependent on Dzungaria following a severe famine in 1723; the Orta Zhuz drifted to Bukhara and submitted to its Emir, and the Alchin Zhuz submitted to the Khiva Khanate. The political unity of Orta Zhuz and the Alchin Zhuz broke up.

The territories populated by nomadic Turkomans were incorporated into the first Moslem states of Central Asia following the Arab conquest, so, like Kazakh people, Turkomans began to adopt Islam as early as the tenth century. From the tenth to the twelfth centuries, Moslem rulers who subjugated the Turkoman tribes built towns in their territories, with fortresses, mosques, *madrasas*, and bazaars. Many Turkomans settled in these towns, notably in Merv. A remarkable architectural monument – the Sultan Sanjara Mausoleum – was built in that town in the twelfth century.

But the nomads did not adopt Islam as their main religion until the period from the sixteenth to the eighteenth century. During that period, northern Turkoman tribes moved to Akhal, the valleys of the Atrek, the Gurgen, and the Amu Darya (after the Amu Darya changed its course and Lake Sarykamysh dried up). By the early nineteenth century, the area populated by the Turkomans was divided between the Bukhara and Khiva khanates, on the one hand, and Iran on the other. However, although they paid taxes and did military service, the nomadic Turkomans were ruled by their tribal leaders – *begs* and *vakils*. Their way of life and lifestyle patterns remained largely unchanged. This is how the Turkomans were described by nineteenth-century Hungarian traveller Vambery: 'The Turkomans are not fanatics ... their idea of the Koran is vague. Their performance of Muhammadan rites is poor.'[16] At that time, religious fanatics were also rare among other nomadic peoples of Central Asia.

The Kirghiz adopted Islam much later than the Kazakh and the Turkomans.[17] They lived in the north-eastern part of Central Asia. in Jetysu within the Pamir-Alai mountain region in the south-west and the Tien Shan mountain range in the north-east, a typical cattle-breeding zone. Khirghiz people never made any attempt to set up a state of their own, and their territories were never incorporated into a Central Asian state.

A traveller who crossed Central Asia on his way to China in 1534 wrote that nomadic Kirghiz were of Mongol origin and did not acknowledge the authority of any sovereign, but only that of their elders, whom they called maliks.[18] According to Moslem sheikhs of Fergana and other states not far from Tien Shan, who often came to the area populated by Kirghiz people in the sixteenth century, the Kirghiz were still, at that time, polytheistic and idol-worshippers. This began to change substantially in the early eighteenth century, when Kirghiz tribes were chased southwards by the Kalmucks and established fairly regular contacts with Fergana, Bukhara, and Kashgaria. It was at that time that Kirghiz noblemen – *manaps* – began to adopt Islam. Kokand khans considered it a high priority to Islamise the Kirghiz and add their territory to the khanate. By the 1830s, most of the territory where the Kirghiz roamed had been added to the Kokand Khanate.

The decisive contribution to the spread of Islam among Kirghiz – and among all nomadic peoples – was made by Sufi sheikhs (*ishans*) and dervishes. They were the first Moslem missionaries in the area (for a long time, there were no others). *Ulama*, if they arrived at all, came much later, so Islamic dogmas and Shariah laws never acquired very deep roots there. The Shariah coexisted with the *Adat*, and Islam with shamanism, worship of saints, and other pre-Islamic religions. Early Islamic egalitarian ideas and Sufism's interpretation of them were in tune with the traditions of tribal democracy. Nomads never observed Islamic prohibitions and laws very closely. They developed Islamic practices of their own, which differed from those existing in urban and rural areas. Their practices were determined by the first Moslems among the nomads and by the preservation of tribal organisation and the nomadic way of life, rather than during the period when Islam was adopted.

The difference between nomadic and settled populations constantly influenced political developments in Central Asia and the political destinies of Central Asian peoples.

The consolidation of a single religion undoubtedly promoted the political unity of the region's states, tribes, nomadic and settled populations. But, despite the dominance of a single religion, many contradictions persisted until the time when Central Asia was incorporated into the Russian Empire, and even after that.

The major ethnic groups then emerging in Central Asia – the Tajiks, the Turkomans, the Uzbek, the Kazakh, and the Kirghiz – were scattered over Central Asia in such a way that every region had enclaves populated by ethnic minorities and none of the khanates remained ethnically homogeneous. This impeded the consolidation of Central Asian states and created numerous sources of tension, some of which still exist today.

Religion was also an important factor in determining the foreign-policy priorities of the Central Asian khanates. The confrontation between Sunnism, the official religion of Central Asia, and Shiism, the official religion of Iran, pushed the region away from Iran and towards Sunni Turkey, whose sultan was considered to the the caliph (spiritual leader) of all faithful Sunnis. Sunni–Shiite contradictions were the main reason for strained relations between Iran and the Bukhara Khanate and even caused clashes between neighbouring villages. It was largely because of that confrontation that Iran never restored its former leadership in Central Asia.

Within each khanate, Islam was undoubtedly an integrating factor. But, taking Central Asia in general, or even the entire Arab-Moslem world, it should be said that, in the whole period since the collapse of the medieval empires, Islam has not brought into being a large united Arab or Central Asian state.

The last attempt to unite the whole of *Ma Wara al-Nahr* in a single Iranian State, and to establish Iranian domination over Central Asia in opposition to the region's links with Ottoman Turkey, was made by Nadir Shah (1736–47). But after his death the large Iranian state disintegrated, and the Central Asian khanates remained independent until Russia established its protectorate over them.

Notes

1. The section 'Central Asia at the Crossroads of the Greatest Cultures of Antiquity' is based on sources gathered and processed by B. G. Gafurov in B. A. Litvinsky (ed.), *The Tajik. A Primeval, Ancient, and Medieval History*, Moscow, 1972, and K. V. Traver, A. Y. Yakubovsky and M. E. Voronets in S. P. Tolstoy *et al.* (eds.), *A History of the Peoples of Uzbekistan* (in Russian), vol. 1, Tashkent, 1959.
2. Narshakhi Abu-Bakr Muhammad, *Tarihi Bukhara (A History of Bukhara)*, trans.

into Russian by N. Lykoshin, Tashkent, 1897. For more information about the Arab conquest of Central Asia see Y. A. Beliaev, *The Arabs, Islam, and the Arab Caliphate in the Early Middle Ages* (in Russian), pp. 190–1, 200–3.

3. This account of the battle, found in Gurek's letter to the Chinese emperor, was regarded as the most reliable one by the prominent Russian orientalist, W. Bartold; see W. Barthold, *On the History of the Arab Conquest of Central Asia; Works* (in Russian), vol. 2, Moscow, 1964.

4. Tolstoy *et al.*, p. 163.

5. Al-Biruni in S. P. Tolstoy (ed.), *A Collection of Articles*, Moscow and Leningrad, 1950.

6. This concept, first formulated by B. A. Litvinsky, is thoroughly analysed by B. G. Gafurov in *The Tajik*, p. 324.

7. L. Monogarova, 'Pagan elements in the Moslem rites of the Ismailis of the Western Pamirs'; I. Mukhiddinov, 'Astral beliefs as mirrored in the lifestyles of the Ismailis of the Western Pamirs' in *Islam and Problems of Inter-civilisational Interaction* (in Russian), Institute of Islamic Civilisation, Moscow, 1992, pp. 124–7, 130–4.

8. Translated from Tolstoy *et al.*, p. 277.

9. J. S. Trimingham, *Sufi Orders in Islam*, trans. into Russian, ed. and foreword by O. F. Akimushkin, Moscow, 1989, p. 61. The information about the wandering dervishes of the Yasaviyah brotherhood is also from the same book, pp. 57 ff.

10. Translated from Tolstoy *et al.*, p. 324.

11. W. Barthold, *Twelve Lectures on the History of the Turkic Peoples of Central Asia; Works* (in Russian), vol. 5, Moscow, 1968, pp. 146–54.

12. Ruy Gonzalez de Clavijo, 'The life and work of Great Tamerlane, by Clavijo. A journal of a travel to the court of Timour in Samarkand in 1403–1406', the original text and translations with notes in I. I. Sreznevsky (ed.), *A Miscellany of the Russian Language and Literature*, Department of the Russian Academy of Sciences, vol. 28, St Petersburg, 1881; see also Tolstoy *et al.*, pp. 345–68; Ahmad ibn Arab Shah, *Tamerlan or Timur the Great Amir*, trans. J. N. Sanders, London, 1936.

13. Translated from M. V. Lavrov, *The Spread of Islam in What is Now Turkestan* (in Russian), Tashkent, 1912, pp. 54–5.

14. Translated from *A History of the Peoples of Uzbekistan* (in Russian), vol. 2 Tashkent, 1947.

15. Translated from A. Mukhtarov, 'The attitude of the clergy of Maverannahr to the establishment of Islam as the official religion of Iran' in *Islam and Problems of Inter-civilisational Interaction*, Institute of Islamic Civilisation, Moscow, 1992, p. 134.

16. A. Vambery, *A Journey over Central Asia* (in Russian), 2nd edn, Moscow, 1867. Journey from Teheran across the Turkmenian desert and along the east shore of the Caspian to Khiva, Bukhara, and Samarkand, made in 1863 by Vambery, a member of the Pest-based Hungarian Academy, with a research grant from the Academy.

17. W. Barthold, *The Kirghiz* (in Russian), Frunze, 1948, pp. 3–39.

18. Ibid.

CHAPTER TWO

ISLAM IN CENTRAL ASIA FROM THE PERIOD OF COLONISATION TO THE 1917 REVOLUTION

The Russian colonisation of Central Asia and Russia's policy with regard to Islam

The incorporation of Central Asia into the Russian Empire in the 1860s and 1870s was preceded by a long period during which Central Asian states and nomadic tribes developed and consolidated economic and political links with Russia. For a long time, Central Asia had been a crossing-point for the economic and political interests of Iran, Turki states, and China. The Arab conquest led to a spiritual estrangement between Buddhist–Confucian China and Moslem Central Asia, which was one of the main reasons why China lost its former political influence in the region. From the thirteenth century, the two main political centres of attraction were Iran and Ottoman Turkey. In the period between the sixteenth and the eighteenth centuries, there emerged a third powerful centre of attraction – Russia – which established strong links with Central Asia. This affected, primarily, the parts of Russia populated by ethnic groups that had adopted Islam (Tatars and Bashkirs). Moslem merchants of the Volga River region and the area west of the Urals found it easier to trade with Central Asian merchants because they had the same religion and because the Tatar and Bashkir languages were similar to Uzbek. For their part, Central Asian merchants were interested in trade with Russia.

From the reign of Peter the Great (1689–1725) onwards, Russia showed increasing interest in economic and political penetration of Central Asia. It established diplomatic relations with Central Asian khanates, and Peter I drew up a plan for their incorporation into Russia. Under that plan, several expeditions were sent to Central Asia. A military expedition led by Bekovich-Cherkasski was sent to build fortresses at the former mouth of the Amu Darya, to coerce the Khan of Khiva 'to loyalty and allegiance to Russia', and to explore the possibility of coercing the Khan ,of Bukhara to allegiance.[1] This expedition was wiped out in Khiva; Bekovich was killed, and his fortresses were destroyed by Turkomans. An expedition led by

Figure 7. Mausoleum Mir Sayyed Bahram (X–XI c.), Karmana, Bukhara *oblast*

Buchgolts to explore a route to Central Asia via Siberia and Florno Benveni's mission to Bukhara were also unsuccessful.

But in the eighteenth century, political forces emerged in Central Asia that were interested in consolidating contacts with Russia. The Kazakh Orta Zhuz and Alchin Zhuz pledged allegiance to the Russian czar in the 1730s; their khans were afraid that their territories could be conquered by Dzungaria and hoped to strengthen their own positions under Russian protection. The speaker of the Russian senate, I. Kirillov supported the admission of the Kazakh states, indicating that 'otherwise we may lose not only many of the newly submitted peoples but also territories with many towns, such as Tashkent and Aral, seeking to come under Russia's dominion and miss the present opportunity to establish control over the provinces of Bukhara and Samarkand and the rich Badakhshan region'.[2]

I. Kirillov led a new Russian expedition sent 'to hoist the Russian flag on the shore of the Aral Sea'. In 1734, the expedition founded Orenburg, which became Russia's military and economic bridgehead for penetration of the Uzbek khanates.

In the first half of the nineteenth century, Russia's economic and political penetration of Central Asia grew more intensive. The factors that led Russia to intensify that penetration included high political tensions in Europe, British penetration of the Central Asian market, and British–Russian rivalry in the Middle East. Russia then tried to use diplomacy to settle misunderstandings in its relations with Central Asian khanates. But its methods were not always effective. Delegations sent by Alexander I failed to persuade Khiva and the Turkomans to establish friendly relations with Russia. In the middle of the nineteenth century, Russia tried to exert military pressure on the Khiva khanate. But the military campaign against Khiva, led by Major-General V. A. Perovsky, Military Governor of Orenburg, in 1839, was unsuccessful.

Russian expeditions sent into Central Asia in the 1840s pursued scientific rather than political aims. But the information gathered during these expeditions by a prominent Russian orientalist, Khanykov, and other scholars, provided some idea of life in the Central Asian khanates and the importance of Islam there. This information helped to forge the Russian administration's policy with regard to Islam following the Russian annexation of Central Asian territories which began with the conquest of Tashkent.

Ulama and sheikhs were divided in their response to the Russian conquest. Most saw the Russians as foreigners and infidels and the khanates as a stronghold of Islam in Central Asia; they therefore supported the khans, who led the local population against Russia because it challenged their authority. But that struggle is not to be compared with the holy wars waged against the British and French colonisers in India and Moslem countries of the Middle East, or in the Caucasus.

As mentioned earlier, the official Islamic authorities were well established in the khanates only, while nomadic tribes were just beginning to develop the structures. In Central Asia, Sufi brotherhoods were much less hostile to the Russians than in the Caucasus. Besides, at first some of the Sunni *ulama* and sheikhs (*ishans*) saw Russia's protection as a powerful factor for promoting unification of Central Asia, for ending wars among tribes and khanates, and for defending them against Dzungaria and Shiite Iran.

It is well known that, in May 1865, when Russian forces were ready to capture Tashkent, Colonel Chernyayev, who was leading the Russian troops, received a deputation of 'honourable enlightened persons' headed by the *Qadi Kolon*, the *mufti*, and the elders of the four districts of the town. A peace treaty was concluded with each district; Chernyayev undertook not to interfere in the town's religious affairs, and presented a gold medal and a velvet robe to the *Qadi Kolon*, on whose initiative the meeting was held and the treaties concluded. Chernyayev then visited the main mosque and principal *madrasas* and even attended classes. The Russian Colonel's obvious desire to win popularity with Moslems derived from his hope that *ulama* would help him to obtain a document stating Tashkent's voluntary submission to the sovereignty of the Russian Emperor. A statement to that effect was drawn up by the *Qadi Kolon*, who had shown pro-Russian tendencies even before the Russians took the town, and was sealed and signed by the elders and other prominent personalities of Tashkent. But the struggle for the town and adjacent territories continued between the Governor-General of Orenburg and the Emir of Bukhara. Only after defeating the Emir did the Governor-General make an official statement about establishing Russia's sovereignty over Tashkent. Territories of the Kokand and Bukhara khanates adjacent to the town were also annexed by Russia. A Turkestan governorship, with Tashkent as its capital, was established in that territory in 1867. The first Governor-General was a military engineer, General K. P. Kaufmann.

The Moslems of the Turkestan Governorship were not granted all the rights of Russian citizens, but continued to be treated as aliens and governed in accordance with special regulations.

The Turkestan Governorship was viewed by the czarist government as an important advance post in Central Asia, intended to promote the conquest of Central Asia and the spread of Russia's influence to countries adjoining the region.

The Bukhara Khan's forces were routed; Khiva put up little resistance, and Russia established its protectorate over the two khanates. Under the treaties concluded with Bukhara in 1868 and 1873, and with Khiva in 1873, the khans had no right to pursue independent foreign policies. Parts of the two khanates' territories were annexed to Russia, and Russian merchants had the right to trade in the khanates on a duty-free basis. But the khans remained quite independent in domestic affairs.

The annexation of Central Asia had mixed consequences: it put the khans in a stronger position in dealing with nomadic tribes, and the treaties with Russia obliged them to eliminate slavery and the slave-trade – an obligation which undeniably promoted Central Asia's economic and social development.

Resistance to the colonisers

As in other parts of the East, resistance to the colonisers was strongest in areas where Islam intermingled with tribal traditions. One graphic example is the difficult conquest of the Turkoman tribes, which had acknowledged for a long time the sovereignty of Khiva and the Kirghiz incorporated into the Kokand Khanate.

The nomadic Kirghiz, who already endured with difficulty the rule of the Kokand Khan, were hostile to the Russian advance towards their territory. A Kirghiz uprising broke out in 1873, headed by Ishaq-mullah Hasan ogly, a Kirghiz of the Margilan district. His allies in the uprising were the ruler of Andizhan (son of Khan Khudayar of Kokand), the ruler of Margilan (the khan's brother) and a Kipchak Khan (son of the former ruler of Kokand put to death by Khudayar). From the very beginning, the forces opposing the khan said they were fighting for the faith.

Ishaq-khan was a *madrasa* student and enjoyed the support of local dervishes. After Khudayar requested Russia's help in the struggle against his opposition and had to flee to Tashkent because the Russians did not come, the insurgents said they were waging a *jihad* against the infidels – the Russians and the apostate khan.

The new khan, Nasreddin, did not side with the rebels, but surrendered Kokand to the Russians and concluded a treaty with Russia that made him 'a humble servant of the Russian Emperor'. Kokand was occupied by Russian troops. The centre of the uprising moved to Andizhan. The rebels proclaimed Ishaq-mullah the ruler of the Kokand Khanate (renaming him Pulat Khan and lifting him on a sheet of white felt, in accordance with the ancient tradition). They even recaptured Kokand, but were soon ejected. The uprising was suppressed by General Mikhail Skobelev in early 1876. On 19 February of that year, the Governor-General of Turkestan ordered the Kokand Khanate to be abolished and reorganised into the Fergana District of Russia. That was the last, and in fact the only, holy war in Central Asia that raised large popular masses against the annexation by Russia, but isolated anti-Russian protests did take place later.

The subjugation of Turkoman territories was not very easy, either. Major problems were posed by local *ishans* and dervishes who strove to unite nomads against the Russians under Islamic slogans. Russia's consolidation in the region was especially important in the view of the aggravation of British–Russian conflicts in the Middle East. Britain was eager to bring Afghanistan into its sphere of influence, to establish control over roads and mountain passes in southern Central Asia which linked the southern Pamirs with its Indian possessions, and to make Central Asia a buffer zone between British and Russian territorial possessions. Conversely, Russia sought to advance deeper into Central Asia, keeping Afghanistan independent and neutral. In early 1884, Russian forces occupied Ashkhabad.

As for Merv, the Russian military authorities managed to persuade its rulers to acquiesce voluntarily to Russia's sovereignty. Britain saw the Russian annexation of Merv as a threat to its positions in the Middle East. The British urged the Afghan Amir Abd-a-Rahman Khan, who had lived in the Turkestan district for a long time before he became ruler of Afghanistan, to lay claims to Turkoman territories; he even made an attempt to occupy the Pendin oasis and the left bank of the River Kushka. But the Afghan forces were driven back to the right bank. The Amir showed no desire to keep on fighting the Russians over Turkoman-populated territories. The conflict was settled, and a peace protocol signed between Russia and Britain in 1885. In accordance with that protocol, a special British–Russian delimitation commission determined the frontier between Russia's Central Asian possessions and Afghanistan, from the Amu Darya to Khorasan in Iran, in 1887. The battle at the Kushka River was the last major military operation resulting from Central Asia's annexation by Russia.

The annexation was completed after the Pamir's delimitation of 1895, when the Pamir mountain region was included in the Russian Empire under a new agreement between Russia and Britain.

In 1886, the Turkestan Governorship was transformed into the Turkestan Territory, and its boundaries were finalised in 1898. The Territory comprised the Trans-Caspian, Samarkand, Semirechye, Syr Darya, and Fergana Regions, and also the vassal principalities of Khiva and Bukhara.

Czarist Russia's Islamic policy

So the Russian state extended its sovereignty over a vast Moslem region. Czarist Russia's policy with regard to Islam in that region was based on long-standing traditions, since there were Moslem enclaves, mainly populated by Tatars and Bashkirs, in Russia proper.

There was the Orenburg Religious Board which was in charge of Islamic affairs in all of Russia, with the exception of Tauria province (which had a Moslem Religious Board of its own). There was also a statute on the Moslem clergy and its jurisdiction. In 1872, the czar endorsed *Regulations for the Management of Religious Affairs* of the Transcaucasian Moslems. Moslem officials subordinated to the Russian authorities enjoyed a number of privileges: they did not pay taxes and nor did their children; the children of clergymen who had served as mosque *imams* or *mudarrises* for 20 years acquired the same rights as the children of noblemen and freemen. Moslem clergymen received *per diem* payments for business trips from the state.[3] The *Regulations* required that the Moslems perform what was prescribed by Islam.

A special code was adopted for the construction of mosques. There were special agencies supervising the construction; mosques were to be built in every community with 200 male Moslems or more. In military districts that had Moslems, there were Moslem chaplains. They were entitled to old-age pensions; if a *mullah* died, a pension was paid to his family. The Oriental Printing House was moved from St Petersburg to Kazan. It printed large numbers of copies of the Koran and other religious books. More religious literature was printed by private printing-houses of Tatarstan.[4]

Following Central Asia's annexation by Russia, similar regulations were adopted by the administration of the Turkestan Governorship. Many of the privileges that Moslem clergymen enjoyed in Russia were extended to Central Asia by order of the Governor-General of Turkestan and the governors of its districts. But these privileges signified subordination of the region's official Islam to the Russian administration.

Sunni officials were always dependent on government authorities. Before the Russian conquest, Sunni clergymen were incorporated into the khanates' government structures and its representatives were dependent on them, too. Now the czarist government tried to discharge the functions formerly performed by Central Asian states with regard to Islam – and even to expand those functions. But Islam was no longer the leading official religion. The people in power were not only foreigners but also non-Moslems, and the state's official religion was Christianity, so Islam's subordination to government structures had an entirely different meaning.

In the first place, the czarist government deprived the *ulama* and sheikhs of some of the land they owned. This land had not only made them rich, but also – more importantly – had given the clergymen, as well as mosques and *madrasas* a certain degree of independence from the ruling powers.

A law enacted in 1886 transferred populated *waqf* land to the ownership of those who cultivated it, and the farmers paid taxes to the state, which allocated money for the upkeep of mosques, *mazars*, and *madrasas* depending on the size of the *waqfs*.

Following the delimitation of Russia and the Bukhara Khanate in 1868, which incorporated Samarkand into the Russian Empire, the mosques and *madrasas* of Turkestan lost the revenues from the *waqfs* in the khanate's territory. Only the two main *madrasas* of Samarkand – the Tilikari and the Shirdar – were permitted by the khan to collect their revenues in the khanate's territory (permission being granted in response to special requests); all the other *madrasas* were denied that right. The Russian authorities did not permit the Bukhara Khanate's religious institutions to collect revenues in Russia's part of the khanate.

New mosques, *maktabs*, and *madrasas* could be built in Turkestan with the permission of the local administration only. The construction of new mosques was subsidised by the Russian Ministry of Internal Affairs. Considerable funds went into these projects. By 1908, Turkestan had 2,571 cathedral mosques, 8,812 parish mosques, 1,211 *mazars* with 1,142 sheikhs, 6,102 *maktabs* for male students and 801 for female students, 336 *madrasas*, and 14,375 other schools; in all, religious schools had 103,377 students.

Most of the schools that existed in the area prior to the 1917 socialist revolution in Russia were religious institutions. *Maktabs* and *madrasas* were run by mosques, and the teachers and *mudarrises* were *ulama*. The schools preserved the system of teaching that had evolved in the period from the ninth to the twelfth century. In *maktabs*, people studied the Koran and books such as the *Chahar Kitaba* (with explanations of the rules of ablution, cognition of faith, legends, and excerpts from the Shariah), the Sufi *Allayar* (a book of religious-mystic poems, published in 1910), and the *Adab al-Salihia* (a code of conduct). *Madrasas* taught subjects related to theology and law (the fundamentals of the Moslem religion, formal logic, the Shariah, and Moslem philosophy) and to general education (metaphysics, cosmography, astronomy, etc.). But according to contemporary reports, general-education subjects were not taught as well in nineteenth-century *madrasas* as they had been in the golden age of Moslem culture in Central Asia.[6] However, the region's annexation by Russia brought to its *madrasas* and *maktabs* printed books that were published in Kazan, and lithographed books made in Tashkent. The work of Turkestan's mosques and *madrasas* was supervised and regulated by the Orenburg Religious Board (Muftiat).

At the turn of the century, there were considerable changes in the system of education. Some *maktabs* and *madrasas* began to teach the Russian language, and the first secular schools for Russians and local nationalities were opened in towns. These were needed to train translators and Russian-speaking local people to work in government offices. The local intellectual élite showed an interest in these schools, too. The schools for Russians and local nationalities certainly helped to build a local intelligentsia, which was then an extremely thin social layer. But there were few such schools. At the start of the twentieth century, only two to three per cent of Central Asia's population could read and write.

One feature of Russia's policy with regard to education and judicature in Central Asia merits special mention. Many Western and Soviet scholars wrote, in the period from the 1930s to the 1950s, that the czarist government had aimed to Russify the Central Asian population from the very outset in order to oust Moslem education and judicature – but that is not true.[6] The czarist government did, however, promote Russianisation of the Empire's colonial regions. In Central Asia, this trend became evident in the late 1900s.

The first moves to promote the spread of the Russian language and Russian education had mixed consequences. On the one hand, the Russian language introduced the local intellectual élite to modern culture. But on the other, it created, under certain circumstances, a confrontation between contemporary and traditional education the latter becoming the main transmitter of Islamic tradition. Russia's

Figure 8. Madrasa Nadir Distep Begi (XVII c.), Bukhara

policy undermined the monopoly of the *ulama* on education. But it should be remembered that Russia's policy in Central Asia did what had been accomplished in Egypt by Muhammad Ali's reforms (in the 1820s–30s), in the Ottoman Empire by the Tanzimat reforms (in 1847), and in other countries by European colonizers.

The inclusion of Central Asia in the Russian Empire introduced an alternative to Islamic education, but it also altered the status of the *mudarrises* (teachers at religious schools): they became dependent on the Russian authorities.

Attitude to Islamic judicature

The policy of the czarist government and the local authorities with regard to Islamic judicature and the status of the *qadis* was somewhat equivocal. We agree with the contemporary Central Asian scholars who disprove the view quite common in Soviet literature – that Russian secular law completely ousted the Shariah and the *adat* in Central Asia following the region's annexation to Russia. The fact is that Shariah courts coexisted with Russian secular courts until 1917. But it is true that the Moslem legal procedure and the application of Shariah precepts were to some extent modernised. Moslem courts changed substantially. In the first place, *qadis*, as well as *biyas* (nomadic people's judges), actually became Russian administration officials. In 1865–7, they were appointed by governors. From 1867 onwards, they were elected by people's representatives.

In 1886, *qadi* courts began to be called people's courts. *Qadis* continued to try cases in accordance with the Shariah, on the basis of *rivoyatas* – statements submitted by plaintiffs and defendants. These statements were drawn up by *muftis* and private attorneys (*vakils*) and examined in court by *ulama* learned in law. Courts were broadly regarded as private institutions, so court officials were paid no salary. *Qadis* did not receive any formal remuneration. They were paid by the parties, and the sums were fixed by custom. Court clerks were paid for every case, and *rivoyatas* were paid for by the parties in question. People's courts remained religious courts, and so, morally unacceptable actions (sins) were regarded as criminal offences; therefore, the Moslem scale of punishment remained in effect. *Qadi* courts were not allowed to use the most extreme types of punishment prescribed by the Shariah. Death sentences and maiming were replaced by fines, imprisonment, or exile to Siberia. The gravest cases were tried on the basis of Russian laws. Crimes against Christianity, offences against the government system, failures to perform duties to the state or to the local authorities, and some other cases, were tried by Russian judges in secular courts (courts of arbitration). Moslem courts were formally subordinate to local authorities, but practically the authorities found it very difficult to supervise their work. One czarist government official admitted that 'the problem of supervising people's courts (*qadi* and *biya* courts) is absolutely impossible to resolve in practice'.[7] In Turkestan, *qadis* always had more rights and powers than in the other Moslem regions of Russia. This was largely because there were considerably fewer educated Moslems in Central Asia than, for instance, in Kazan; very few Russian administration officials meanwhile spoke Oriental languages, so they had only a very vague idea of the Shariah. The first works on Moslem law written in

Russian were published as late as the beginning of the twentieth century. They included: *The Sharia Court* by Tsvetkov (1911) and *The Sharia* by Ostroumov (1909).

At the same time, the selection of candidates and the appointment of mosque *imams, mudarrises,* and *qadis* remained a prerogative of the Russian administration. The *Qadi Kolon* and the Sheikh ul-Islam of Tashkent were formally appointed by the Governor-General, and *muftis* – the heads of Moslem Religious Boards – by royal decree.[8]

Pilgrimages to Mecca and Medina were also controlled by the state. The czarist government encouraged, organised, and even paid for the pilgrimages. It set up a Society for Moslem Pilgrim's Affairs, subordinate to the Ministry of Internal Affairs. The Society had the exclusive right to receive and assist those who wanted to make a *hajj*. Moslem pilgrims were given the same assistance as Christian pilgrims going to Jerusalem. The Moslems of Central Asia enjoyed the same benefits as the Moslems of other regions. At the beginning of the twentieth century, 9,000–10,000 people from the Russian Empire went on a *hajj* every year.

The czarist government's policy with regard to Moslem pilgrimages, as well as Moslem education and judicature, shows that the government endeavoured to preserve certain Moslem institutions and even supported them financially, seeking at the same time to establish control over their activities.

It was not easy to control or supervise *ishans* and dervishes. In the middle of the nineteenth century, the Naqshbandiyah brotherhood became notably more active in Turkestan. There were also Vaisis – members of a brotherhood founded in Kazan in 1862 by Bahaadin Vaisov. Vaisov's teaching combined Sufi mysticism with Russian socialism, so it had a considerable following in the lower strata of society.

Mosque *imams, mullahs, qadis,* and *mudarrises* were in some respects highly dependent on the local authorities, but their attitudes to that dependence varied; not all of them submitted to the Russian domination, and very few followed every rule imposed by the authorities. Although they accepted pay and had to tolerate supervision from the Russian authorities, *ulama* sought to preserve their religious independence. Sermons delivered in mosques, *madrasas,* and *maktabs* promoted religious isolationism of Moslems, popularised the Shariah as the only real law, and did not always feature loyalty to the Russian authorities, not even in form. It should be pointed out here that the authorities were aware of the Moslem clergy's real sentiments, even as they tried to render them useful to Russia. In September 1867, the first Governor-General of Turkestan, Kaufmann, wrote to the Defence Minister, D. A. Miliukov, that the

Moslems showed, 'so much cool reserve, so much indifference and even disrespect for representatives of the supreme power that one suspects the existence of some anti-Russian slogan'.[9]

In 1899, after Pulat Khan's uprising was suppressed, the Governor-General of Fergana reported that 'the Moslems' submission is purely superficial, they are still far from the end of the evolution of adapting to the new ruling regime'. He stressed the need to monitor what was preached by *imams* and *mudarrises*, because Moslem clergymen were especially hostile to Russia. To establish control over the *ulama* and restrict their hostile activities, he thought it necessary to 'recognise and legalise Moslem religious organisations – as they were by the wise Ivan the Terrible during the conquest of the Kazan Khanate'.[10]

A prominent Russian statesman, Pyotr Stolypin, Russia's Minister of Internal Affairs and later Prime Minister (in 1907–11), pointed out in one letter that there existed a Moslem problem in the Russian Empire, and that it posed a major threat to the country's internal stability.[11]

So the czarist government was extremely cautious about the establishment of Moslem religious boards in Central Asia. No special board for Central Asia was ever established in czarist Russia. This probably reflected the government's reluctance to increase its interference in the region's religious affairs, or its fear that the establishment of a special religious board for Central Asia would strengthen Islam's position there – or both.

It should be noted that the first Governor-General of Turkestan always opposed the subordination of the territory to any of the existing religious boards and said that a special board had to be established for the region. A commission was set up to draw up a plan for it and a design was worked out but never became reality. Following the suppression of the uprising in Andizhan in 1898, the government drafted *Provisional Regulations for the Management of the Religious Affairs, Schools, and Waqfs of the Moslems of Turkestan Territory* and a new plan to set up a religious board for the Turkestan District, but the plan was never implemented.

In 1905 the Cabinet of Ministers spoke in favour of establishing a Moslem Religious Board of the Turkestan Kray. But a special conference on religious affairs decided against changing the established system of managing religious affairs in Turkestan.

Islam in the steppes

The status of Islam in the urban and permanent-population rural communities of the Turkestan territory (kray) was quite different from that which it had in steppe areas populated by numerous nomadic peoples that still lived in tribes (Kazakh, Kirghiz, and Turkomans).

The Russian authorities did not interfere with the nomads' use of the *adat*, since it had been mixed with Islamic precepts for a long time, and the spread of Islam in the steppes was promoted by the authorities.

It is interesting to quote, in this connection, a czarist government official who was instructed to explore the situation of Kirghiz people soon after their territory was annexed by Russia. He wrote that the country's 'political interests required consolidation of the belief in the Kirghiz people and the whole of Central Asia that their religion was inviolable. That and the desire to win over the khans of the steppes led our government not only to show an entirely tolerant attitude to Islam in the initial period, but even to give it some support.'[12]

A State Commission for Religious Affairs was formed following the annexation of nomad-populated steppe areas by Russia, to explore ways of promoting the adoption of Christianity by nomads, starting with the Kazakh. The Commission recommended not interfering directly in Moslem religious affairs, but restricting the spread of Islam among nomads in the future. For his part. K. P. Kaufmann was strongly against conducting Christian missionary work in the steppe areas. He insisted that Moslem *ulama* and sheikhs should have the opportunity to pursue their missionary work among nomads. The Orenburg Muftiat also contributed to the establishment of Islam among the Kirghiz, the Kazakh, and other nomadic peoples, by helping to build mosques and *madrasas* in steppe areas.[13]

Although they made no efforts to impede Moslem missionary activities or the establishment of Islam among nomads, the Russian authorities endeavoured to cultivate pro-Russian sentiments in the nomads' leaders, especially the leaders of the Kazakh people. They volunteered to protect the Kazakh against 'Tatarisation and Turkestanisation', and opened Russian schools for Kazakh; young Kazakh noblemen were admitted to military schools and became commissioned officers in the Russian army. As a result, pro-Russian sentiments were quite strong among the tribal leaders and educated Kazakh people until Russian settlements began to be established in the Kazakh steppe areas. The first local enlighteners in the region were Kazakh; they emerged in the middle of the nineteenth century and at first advocated pro-Russian sentiments.

But as the Russians colonised the nomad-populated steppes, the religious situation and the nomad's attitude to Russia gradually changed.

The czarist government did not encourage the establishment of Russian settlements in Central Asia until the annexation of the region was complete. The decision to let land in the Central Asian steppes to settlers from Russia came in the late 1880s. The first waves of Russian and Ukrainian settlers moved into Kazakh steppes and areas populated by nomadic Kirghiz in the early 1890s.

But for a long time, Russia's resettlement policy was restrained by the government's fear of local revolts and the absence of vacant irrigated land. A new dimension was added to that policy around 1910. In the period between 1907 and 1917, the Central Asian policy was discussed repeatedly by the Duma. It passed a number of laws on a plan prepared by Count Konstantin Palen and a memorandum written by Alexander Krivoshejn, the Minister of Agriculture, which were in line with Stolypin's reforms. The new dimension concerned resettlement of efficient Russian farmers, and the purposes of the resettlement were 'to build a strong popular bulwark on the state's external frontiers and to spread Slavic culture among the Turki-Mongol masses'.[14]

According to statistics for 1911, Russians accounted for 3.7 per cent of Turkestan's population. The number of settlements grew rapidly. By 1914, there were one million settlers in Kazakh steppes alone; they began to oust nomads from their pastures, posing a real threat to their way of life.[15]

The Russians brought the Orthodox faith to Central Asia. The religion, formerly represented by a few adherents – Russian officials, scholars, and travellers – was now professed by large Russian communities. Christian churches were built and Russian Orthodox clergymen came to the area. No Christians ever conducted missionary work there on a meaningful scale, and the Orthodox faith – the official religion of Russia – was never imposed on Central Asia. Local people who adopted Christianity did so voluntarily, and most of those who did were educated people. It was a new phenomenon, however, for Moslems to have to tolerate coexistence with Christianity in their territory; another important factor was that Orthodox Christianity, professed by a tiny minority of the Central Asian population, was the official religion of the state to which Central Asia had been annexed.

Islamic and Russian cultures interacted in most unusual ways. Russian settlements failed to affect the lifestyles of neighbouring Moslem communities. Many towns were clearly divided into two sections: one inhabited by the native population, and the other by Russians. But, unavoidably, their cultures were in close contact and influenced each other – a phenomenon which occurs in any colony.

This can be illustrated by life in Tashkent at the turn of the century, as described by A. I. Dobrosmislov, who studied life in Russia's Moslem provinces for twenty years, in his book *Tashkent Yesterday and Today* (published in 1912).

Figure 9. Minaret Kalyan (XII c.), Bukhara

When the military governorship of Turkestan was established, Tashkent became the seat of its governors, accommodating the territory's military, administrative, judicial, financial, and other agencies. It was also the chief town of the Syr Darya Region. At the turn of the century, the Moslem section of Tashkent had more than 141,000 inhabitants, and the Russian section about 50,500. Most of Tashkent's Moslems were Sart Kalmyk (settled Uzbek) or Kirghiz. (The Russians at that time used the word with reference to both Kirghiz and Kazakh.) There were also many baptized soldiers' children patronized by military agencies, Jews, and people of mixed ancestry. Following all-Russia Moslem Congresses (see below), a Moslem educational society, Pomoshch (Assistance), was set up in Tashkent. The leading role in the education of Moslems there, and in most of Central Asia, was then played by Tatars.

Teachers came from Russia to work at the Russian schools. Some of them were Christian missionaries, and that, according to Dobrosmislov, 'caused animosity among the local population and harmed the Russian schools' prestige'.

There were 333 mosques in the Moslem part of Tashkent and 16 in the Russian section; there were about 20 Russian Orthodox churches, most of them in the Russian section. At the end of 1884, the first school for Russians and local nationalities was opened in the Moslem section of Tashkent, to teach the Russian language to local children. Dobrosmislov writes that students for the school were recruited under pressure from the authorities. Tashkent's *maktabs* had a total of 7,503 pupils.

After 1905, there was an appreciable revival in the religious, political, and cultural life of the Moslem part of Tashkent.

Islam in the khanates of Bukhara and Khiva

In accordance with the treaties that formalised Russia's protectorate over Central Asia, the khanates' religious affairs were considered their internal affairs and were not be supervised by the Russian authorities. Islam remained the khanates' official religion and an inseparable part of their state structures. The khans were the secular and the religious leaders of their states. *Ulama* and *ishans*, *madrasas* and mosques retained their *waqfs* and a certain degree of independence from the ruling powers. *Zakat* was no longer a voluntary contribution but a compulsory state tax. The well-being of Islamic officials and *ishans* depended largely on the khan, but the khan was dependent on them, too, because they shaped public opinion. The khan's prestige and authority were largely determined by his religious orientation.

Bukhara greatly honoured the Sultan of Turkey – the caliph of all Sunni Moslems. The Khan of Bukhara enjoyed great respect in the entire Moslem world, too. This was largely because Bukhara had been famous for centuries as a centre of Moslem theology and philosophy. But the Khan was respected mainly for his huge wealth: at the start of the twentieth century, the Khan had 27 million gold roubles deposited at the State Bank of Russia and about 7 million roubles at private banks. Besides, the Khan was the world's third biggest seller of Karakul furs. Without the knowledge of czarist Russia's diplomats, the Khan donated several hundred thousand gold roubles for the construction of the Hejaz railway line (from Asia Minor to Medina), which was built by the Sultan of Turkey with German support. However, there is no doubt that Russia's protectorate weakened Bukhara's traditional links with the rest of the Moslem world, and that, in turn, caused discontent among Bukhara's *ulama* and *ishans*.

Bukhara's reorientation was also promoted by the extension of the Trans-Caspian railway line to Cardzou, Bukhara, and Samarkand. The line ran across the Zeravshan River Valley, where caravans had travelled for centuries from Bukhara to Samarkand, Tashkent, Balkh, Kabul, and Herat, then on to Kandahar and Meshed. Caravan trade was controlled by Bukhara merchants, many of whom had long-established links with *ulama* and *ishans*. The railway line changed all this. Russian settlements that emerged at railway stations gradually developed into small towns, with Russian schools and churches.

Russian joint-stock companies were granted land concessions in the Bukhara Khanate, and Russian forces were stationed on the border with Afghanistan. The first local industrialists were Bukharan Jews. But even among Moslem merchants, there emerged bourgeois elements who directed their interests towards Russia and favoured modernisation of society. This bourgeois component, and especially the stratum of people educated at local Russian schools and new-style *maktabs* and *madrasas* (where the Russian language was taught), produced Bukhara's first reform-minded politicians.

Khan Abdulahad, who ruled Bukhara at the beginning of the twentieth century, was awarded the rank of Cavalry-General of the Russian Army, the court rank of Adjutant-General, the honorary rank of Cossack chieftain, etc. His heir was educated in Russia; he was awarded the rank of aide-de-camp to the Emperor and the title of Prince. The Khan himself was not particularly enthusiastic about reform. The Russian authorities in Turkestan believed that the Khan's independence in internal affairs impeded reform. But as he began to direct his interests towards Russia, the Khan understood that, to achieve close relations with Russia he would have to alter the khanate's regime, making it similar to the Russian one, which would certainly be a major step towards modernisation. But the plans to modernise society drew an angry response from the *ulama* and *ishans*.

The revolution of 1905 in Iran and the enactment of a constitution in that country in 1906 had a profound impact on Bukhara. But the Young Turks' revolution and the overthrow of Sultan Abdul-Hamid II in 1909 came as a real shock to the ruling groups and Islamic officials of Bukhara. There were disturbances in Kukyab and Hisar districts, with demonstrations led by *ulama* in Kulyab and Shahrisiabz. *Ulama* called on people to condemn the developments in Iran and Turkey, as well as reform in Bukhara, and to act in defence of Islam. It took the Khan's forces three days to being the towns under control.

In January 1910, an Islamicist mass movement against the Khan led to a clash between Sunnis and Shiites in Bukhara. Sunnis, who made up an absolute majority of the khanate's population, openly revolted against the Khan's *kushbegi*, Astanakul, whose mother was a native of

Iran. The revolt was caused by the *kushbegi*'s granting of permission for the celebration of the Shiite holiday, *Ashura*, throughout Bukhara. (Previously the celebrations had been restricted to the Iranian section of the town.) As a Shiite procession moved along the main streets of Bukhara, Sunnis taunted the rite and insulted the Shiites. A group of Shiites attacked a crowd of Sunnis, killing one of them. This triggered a terrible massacre of Iranians. Many sought refuge under the protection of Russian troops. About 500 Bukharans and Iranians were killed in the massacre. Bloodshed stopped only after Russian troops and the Khan's forces were sent into the town and the *kushbegi* was dismissed. The Russian military command helped to organise a reconciliation ceremony, which was attended by Sunni and Shiite *ulama*.[16] But a latent war between Bukhara's Islamic officials and advocates of reform persisted until the dramatic events of 1917.

In the Khanate of Khiva, the influence of Islam on the political situation was no less complex and controversial. Russia's relations with Khiva were somewhat different from its relations with Bukhara. Under the Treaty of 1873, the khanate's territory on the right bank of the Amu Darya, with its settled and nomadic peoples, was to be annexed to Russia (article 33). The Amu Darya District was established in that territory. Its governor was the diplomatic representative of the governorship-general to the Khiva Khan's court. The district's Islamic authorities were placed under Russia's direct control. But the government system, and lifestyles of the khanate proper, retained many features of the patriarchal tribal organisation inherited from nomadic peoples. So the lifestyles and customs of the Khiva court differed from those of Bukhara. It was not uncommon to see a campfire burning in the middle of the Khan's Council Room (just as in a nomad's tent). When the weather became just warm enough in spring, the Khan ordered a large white-felt tent to be put up in his garden and lived there till winter. But the main difference was that the Khan of Khiva examined people's complaints personally, in accordance with the ancient tradition – and that certainly diminished the importance of the *qadis* in society. The leading role in the khanate's political affairs was played by Sufi orders, not by established Islam.

At the end of the nineteenth century, the Khan of Khiva and his supporters still clung to hopes of regaining the independence they had enjoyed. In 1881, the Khan sent an envoy to Afghanistan, with a letter calling on Amir Abd-ar-Rahman Khan to lead a united movement of faithful Moslems against Russia. Abd-ar-Rahman Khan at that time avoided conflicts with Russia and refused to ally with Khiva. During the conflict between Russia and Afghanistan at the Kushka River in 1885, the Khiva court seriously considered the possibility of striking against Russia.

For a long time, Russia's influence on life in Khiva was not as pronounced as its influence on Bukhara. Khiva was very far from Russia's cultural centres; there were no major Russian settlements and few Russians in its territory, so the local people did not object to the Russians as much as the Bukharans did.

At the start of the twentieth century, the situation began to change. Conflicts among towns and between settled and nomadic Uzbek and especially Turkomans led the Khans of Khiva to seek Russia's support.

Khan Muhammad Rahim II (1865–1910) opposed innovations but his son, Khan Isfediar, adopted a different attitude. His enthronment edict proclaimed the course of modernisation of society and social reform. The reform was carried out by the Khan's young Prime Minister, Islam Khoja, who was strongly influenced by Tatar Moslem reformers. He had visited Moscow and St Petersburg and was familiar with Stolypin's reforms and Russian culture. Khoja's reforms drew a negative response from dogma-ridden *ulama* and *ishans* and met with bitter resistance from nomadic Turkomans. Formerly, they had paid no regular taxes, but the reform imposed such taxes on them, to be levied on a per tent basis. Their revolt against the Khan was led in 1914 by Qurban Mamed. He succeeded in uniting Turkoman tribes for a while; one of the strongest tribes, the Janayad, even proclaimed him Janayad Khan. He was supported by Khan Ishan, the most popular of the Sufi *ishans*, who became Janayad Khan's adviser and stayed with him until 1924.

In the first quarter of the twentieth century, the *ishans* were actually the main political force in the Khiva Khanate. The Sufi brotherhoods, *Naqshbandiyah* and *Qubraviyah*, had networks of local people covering the khanate's entire territory: urban and rural areas and territories populated by nomads.[17] Apart from Khan Ishan, the central figure among the *ishans* of Khiva proper was Muhammad Yousoufjan. In the spring of 1914, he returned to Khiva from Mecca, where he had built a *tekke* (a hostel) for *hajjis* from Khiva. The money for the project was donated by rich inhabitants of Khiva, including the Khan. Muhammad Yousouf was a highly influential person in Khiva and was declared a *khazrat* (a saint). *Ishans* said that the Khan's modernisation policy (including the introduction of electricity, cinemas, and telephones – previously unknown in Khiva) was against the Shariah. They plainly linked the innovations with the Russian orientation of the Khan and his close associates. The opposition of the *ishans* destabilised the khanate until 1917.

The nomadic Turkomans, meanwhile, launched a *jihad* against the Khan. In 1916, they captured Khiva, killed the Prime Minister, seized the Khan, and took a huge ransom for sparing his life and that of his harem, then returned to the steppes.[18]

The government of Russia, which generally preferred not to intervene in conflicts between khans and nomads or among khans, then decided that the balance of power in the khanate had been upset and that Russia's position was jeopardised. Punitive Russian forces were sent to Turkmenia, and the uprising was suppressed. The leader of the Turkoman uprising, Janayad Khan, fled to Iran and did not return to Turkmenia until 1918.[19]

Not all the *ishans* and *ulama* opposed modernisation of Central Asia. Even in the khanates, to say nothing of the territories actually annexed to Russia, a considerable number of well-educated people emerged just before World War I: they were Islamic reformers, enlighteners, and local nationalists advocating reform and pinning their hopes on Russia. Some advocated secular goals while others were *ulama* favouring reform. Moslem reformers spread through Central Asia the religious movement of Russia's Moslems known in history as Jadidism.

The Jadidists

As in the rest of the Orient, new-style, bourgeois religious reforms spread in Central Asia at the same time as enlightenment. It is difficult to identify, as Alexandre Benigsen suggests, the consecutive phases in the development of national self-consciousness of the Moslems in Central Asia, i.e. religious reform, cultural reform, and political reform. Most people who advocated a reform of Islam in accordance with the changes brought about by Central Asia's annexation to Russia also promoted enlightenment. The advocates of cultural reform constantly stressed the need to modernise Islam. Some of the religion and culture reformers became Central Asia's first nationalists.

We have seen that in Central Asia freethinking always coexisted with Islam, and confrontation occurred during periods of decline and crisis of Moslem culture. This fact was reflected in Islam's position in Central Asian societies and in the nature of religious reforms. Secular enlightenment was promoted mainly by educated Kazakh, as was understandable. Dogmatic Islam never acquired very deep roots among nomads, and Islam in general was dominated by Sufism and trends towards religious syncretism – a synthesis of Islam, tribal institutions, and pre-Islamic beliefs. And also, the few representatives of Moslem societies' upper classes who adopted Christianity were Kazakh.

The first Kazakh enlightener was Chokan Velikhanov (1835–65), a tribal nobleman and direct descendant of Genghis Khan. Velikhanov had a brilliant education at Russian schools and colleges and became a well-known ethnographer. He strove hard to promote Central Asia's unification with Russia and to bring Russian and Asian cultures closer together. He believed that only Russia could lead Central Asian peoples along the path of progress and protect them from Tatar merchants' competition and the obscurantism and dogmatism of Bukharan *ulama*. 'Without the Russians we are only Asiatics,' he wrote.[20] Velikhanov took a secular view of Islam. He believed that Islam had no deep roots among Kazakh people and played a conservative role in Central Asia's life and cultural development, impeding the spread of Russian culture in the region. In a letter to the Russian government, Velikhanov wrote: 'We insist that the government should not provide protection to a religion hostile to any [kind of] knowledge.'[21]

But Velikhanov's position with regard to Islam was not typical of nineteenth-century and early twentieth-century Central Asian enlighteners. Most of them assumed religious positions. They all criticised dogmatic *ulama* and religious fanaticism, but they did not aim to being down Islam. On the contrary, they sought the most effective ways of modernising it, to help it to survive in the emerging bourgeois cultural environment, which was new to the Moslem regions of Russia.

Moslem reformers

The first Moslem reformers were Tatars, but many of them worked in Central Asia. The best known of these are Abunaer al-Qursavi, who lived and worked in the early nineteenth century, and Mullah Shehabaddin ibn Bahaaddin, known in historical literature as al-Marjani (1818–89).

Al-Qursavi was educated at the Bukhara *madrasa*. He was one of the first to stress the need to reform Islam, protesting against unquestioning submission to the *taqlid* and advocating the right to independent opinions (*ijtihad*). The *ulama* of Bukhara, most of whom were traditionally dogmatic, condemned his speeches as heresy. On the Khan's orders, al-Qursavi was sentenced to death in 1813. He managed to escape, first to Samarkand and then to Kazan, where he led another religious reformist movement. The *ulama* of Kazan, who had close links with those of Bukhara, also accused him of violating Islamic precepts. Al-Qursavi was in danger again, so he left for Arabia. He died in Constantinople.

Al-Qursavi's followers were persecuted both in Kazan and in Central Asia. But some *ulama* supported al-Qursavi. One of these was al-Marjani. He advocated a religious reform, whose major elements can be summed up as follows: (1) let every Moslem find his own answers in the Koran to questions about religion; (2) put an end to the tradition of unquestioning submission; (3) remove old dogmatic

Figure 10. Madrasa Miri Arab (XV c.), Bukhara

scholastic books from *madrasas*; (4) introduce the teaching of the Koran, *hadith*, and the history of Islam *madrasas*; (5) permit the teaching of secular science and the Russian language at *madrasas*; and (6) bring the Moslems back to the roots of early Islamic culture.

Al-Marjani spent a long time hiding in Samarkand from the Khan of Bukhara. Here he met Qadi Abu Said, a well-educated man advocating progressive ideas. He had a large library, and al-Marjani studied works by al-Qursavi, whose ideas he developed in his programme, and by Ibn Sina and other great thinkers of the past. Al-Marjani developed their views in his programme of reforms. The first two of the programme's six major provisions were based entirely on the Moslem rationalists' thesis that man explores the universe and God with his intelligence. His calls to permit the teaching of secular science at *madrasas* accorded with ancient thinkers' ideas about the need to study mathematics, astronomy, natural science, geography, medicine, and other sciences of universal significance.

One of al-Marjani's prominent contemporaries was Ahmad, son of Nosir, known in Tajik literature by the pseudonyms Ahmad Donish ('knowledgeable Ahmad') or Ahmad Qalla ('brainy Ahmad' 1827–97). He was one of the most fascinating enlighteners of Central Asia. Like al-Marjani, he grew up and was educated in a religious environment. His father was the *imam* of a district mosque in Bukhara. Ahmad completed a course at Bukhara's **Miri Arab madrasa** where he had a cell of his own.

But, unlike al-Marjani, Ahmad did not devote his life to theology. He was the first to protest against the obsolete teaching system: he refused to teach at a *maktab* – even though he had the rank of *mudarris* – in order to express disapproval of the obsolete teaching methods adopted at that school. Ahmad was famous as one of Bukhara's best-educated people and taught astronomy, geography, mathematics, history, and more secular subjects to a group of disciples in Tajik, his native language. He did not deny the role of Islam in the development of Central Asian culture, as did Velikhanov, but endeavoured to revive the traditions of freethinking established by his great ancestors. He was a scholar and philosopher, but also a remarkable poet and writer, 'the father of modern Tajik literature'[22]. In his treatise *On Mutual Assistance and Civilisation*, Ahmad Donish puts the question: 'What was man created for?', and tries to answer it on the basis of the Koran. He was one of the first Central Asian enlighteners to try to use Islam to substantiate the need for political reform and constitutional forms of government in the Central Asian khanates.[23]

Ahmad Donish's progressive ideas were similar to, or identical with, the views of another remarkable thinker, the Kazakh enlightener Abai Kunanbaev (1845–1904).

Kunanbaev's views featured a close combination of enlightenment and religious reformism. He was an outstanding representative of Central Asia's Moslem nomads and of Central Asia in general.

A strong advocate of Central Asia's orientation towards Russia, fully aware of the importance of Russia's cultural mission in the east and fascinated by the ideas of the Russian progressive thinkers of the last quarter of the nineteenth century, Kunanbaev had an ardent passion for his people's original culture and considered Islam an inalienable part of that culture. Abai believed in the great value of the foundations of Islam but was against dogmatisation or absolutism in their interpretations by theologians. He maintained that Islam should be combined with his people's pre-Islamic customs and beliefs, as well as with Russia's progressive thought, and that thought and research should be free from religious restrictions. He criticised *mullahs* and *ulama* who resisted change, but showed a deep respect for the wisest of them, and always emphasised that Islam was basically intended to establish justice and did not prohibit adoption of other cultures' achievements.

The ideas of al-Marjani, Ahmad Donish, and Abai Kunanbaev were furthered in Jadidism, an enlightening movement that began with the popularisation of a new teaching method, *usul-i jadid*, which gave the movement its name.

The new method comprised phonetic teaching of Arabic and commented reading of texts that explained the world. The *maktabs* using the new method were called 'new-method' schools.

Jadidism was founded by Ismail-bek Gasprinski (1851–1914) who had a profound effect on the thinking of educated Moslems both in Russia and in Central Asia. His followers and supporters formed the core of the Jadid movement, which produced the founders and leaders of the first modern-style Moslem political parties and Moslem nationalist organisations. His life was typical of that of Moslem ideologists and public figures of the period.

Ismail-bek Gasprinski was born in Ajikoi Village not far from Bakhchisarai in the Crimea. His father, Mustapha Gasprinski, was an innkeeper. In 1853 (i.e. after Ismail was born), Mustapha Gasprinski was commissioned junior-lieutenant, and his name was put on the gentry family register. After studying at a village *maktab*, Ismail entered a Russian school in Voronezh, then a military school in Moscow. At the age of 14, he left the military school and travelled on foot from Moscow to the Crimea. Ismail and a fellow cadet journeyed from Moscow to the Volga and the Don, then crossed the Azov Sea to Bakhchisarai. Ismail studied at the Zinjerli *madrasa* there for about three years, then went to Constantinople, 'to acquire higher knowledge', then moved to Paris. There he worked for a press advertising agency, writing advertisements in several languages, including Arabic, Persian, and Turkish. At one time, he worked as a secretary for the Russian classic author, Ivan Turgenev, who at that time lived in Paris. In France, Gasprinski wrote his first articles for Russian newspapers. He returned to the Crimea by way of Algeria, Tunisia, Egypt, and Greece. In 1881 in Simferopol, Gasprinski published his first work, entitled: *The Moslems of Russia. Thoughts, Notes, and Observations of a Moslem.* In 1883, he founded a newspaper of his own, *Tercuman* (Interpreter). The publication was praised by al-Marjani and received financial support from the brothers Z. and L. Ramiev, Tatar businessmen involved in gold-mining. From 1870 to February 1917, there were about 435 Moslem periodicals published in Turkic languages in Russia; most were local and did not appear regularly. But *Tercuman* was published regularly from 1883 to 1914 and was very popular with Moslems, not only in Russia, but also in many other countries.[24]

In his first work *The Moslems of Russia*, in articles published in *Tercuman,* and in numerous later works, Gasprinski outlined his views as an enlightener. He maintained that the incorporation of large Moslem-populated territories into Russia was good for Islam. He rejected the view of dogmatic *ulama* that Russia was 'a hostile state' (*darul harb*) to Moslems. He wrote that the Moslem khanates of Ryazan, Kazan, Astrakhan, Siberia, the Crimea, the Transcaucasus, and Central Asia had been incorporated into Russia 'at times of historical necessity' and that the transfer of huge Moslem populations with their rich territories 'under Russia's sovereignty and protection

. . . makes Russia the natural intermediary between Europe and Asia, knowledge and ignorance, progress and stagnation'.[25]

Gasprinski's enlightenment-related views about the need for secular education and changes in the status of Moslem women were closely linked with his ideas about modernising Islam and Islamic education.

Like al-Marjani, Gasprinski believed that every Moslem had the right to read the Koran and the Sunna to find his own answers to questions about religion, but he also extended that right to social issues. He said that, in exploring natural and social phenomena, people should be guided by rationalism, observation, personal experience, and common sense. Like most Moslem reformers in the east at the turn of the century, Gasprinski objected to the interpretation of Islam as divine predestination and advocated free will for active people. In his newspaper, Gasprinski called on people to be active, quoting a *hadith* with the Prophet's words: 'One day devoted to public service pleases Allah more than forty days of fasting and forty nights of praying.'[26]

Gasprinski developed the new method of teaching – *usul-i jadid*. In 1884, he founded the first *maktab* that employed the new method and wrote the first new-method school book for it. At the same time, he proposed a reform of *madrasa* education and requested Russian experts to help the Moslems to carry it out. The reform was to introduce new general education subjects (geography, history, natural science, arithmetic and planimetry, pedagogics, Russian law, and the Russian language). Gasprinski proposed that the new *madrasas* be classified first-rate and staffed with graduates of the Oriental Studies Department of Moscow University or the Lazarev Institute of Oriental Languages. Gasprinski attached great significance to the reform. 'The influence of *madrasas* on a Moslem society, the entire system of its life and thought, is much stronger and more direct than the influence of any university on a European society. *Maktabs* and *madrasas* – institutions with roots grown deep into the Moslem soil, rather than lying on the surface, like foreign schools – enjoy Moslems' great respect, sympathy, and trust and are hallowed by age-old traditions.'[27]

Gasprinski's reformist views and enlightening activities were condemned by conservative *ulama*, kadimists (derived from the Arabic word *kadim*, meaning 'ancient'), and by some Christian missionaries, who favoured Russianisation of Moslems. One of them, N. I. Ilminsky, was strongly against the enlightenment of Moslems and constantly opposed Gasprinski. An active campaign against Gasprinski was launched in the paper *Din ve magishat* ('Faith in Life'), a publication of the kadimists (they were also called the Old Believers in Russia) that appeared in Orenburg from 1907 onwards.

W. Barthold, who visited several Moslem centres of Russia in 1913, wrote that, although the Russian authorities sympathised with the kadimists and considered them to be loyal to Russia, 'the reforms are developing successfully everywhere'.[28]

Gasprinski's ideas were popular in Central Asia, too. In Samarkand, the first new-method *madrasa* was founded by Abdul Kadyr Shakuri in1903. His experience led a group of educated Bukharans to set up a new-method *maktab* in their town. In 1905, there were several such schools and a Jadidist secret society ('Children's Education' Society) there. One of its members, and Central Asia's first Jadidist, was Saddriddin Ayni. He was a graduate of the *madrasa* where Ahmad Donish had been educated, and also had the rank of *mudarris*. In Soviet times, Ayni came to be recognised as the founder of modern Tajik literature. His memoirs portray Bukhara's religious and cultural life in that period. He describes the Jadidist secret society's programme aims as being to: '(1) popularise education, help everyone who is eager to learn, create modern literature, encourage people to read periodicals and ethical and educational books; (2) agitate against rites based on ignorance and obscurantism and explain that obscurantism is against the Shariah; (3) agitate against the emir and the ruthlessness of his officials and judges.'[29]

The Jadidists stressed the need for several languages to be studied at *maktabs*. A Jadidist leader, Mahmud Khoja Behbudi, explained the necessity as follows: children should know a Turkic language (Uzbek), to speak in their families [this applied to Bukhara]; Persian (Tajiki) – the language of poetry and culture; Arabic – the language of their religion; Russian – to use for promoting economic and industrial development, and lastly, a European language – English, French, or German – to communicate with the rest of the world.

As in Russia, the Jadidists in Central Asia met with fierce opposition from the kadimists and the emir, who was then considered the leader of all the faithful Moslems. The Jadidists were viewed as criminals acting against Islam. Nevertheless, there were many *mullahs* and *ulama* among them.[30]

Benigsen notes that the Jadidists never managed to prevail over the kadimists in Central Asia up to the dramatic events of 1918. Whether that is true is difficult to say today. But it is well known that debates and conflicts between them affected the entire religious and cultural atmosphere in the Bukhara Khanate and the Turkestan Territory just before, and during World War I. There were 92 new-method *maktabs* in the district in those years, 35 of them in the four major towns of Tashkent, Andizhan, Kokand, and Samarkand. The Jadidists grew rapidly in both number and influence on Bukhara's political life.

In Central Asia, Jadidism was an enlightening movement – and the region's first political ideology. As an ideology, it developed in the first two decades of the twentieth century. The first Moslem political organisations were established around that time, too. The political activity in Central Asia was part of the national liberation take-off then observed in all oriental countries. The Moslem movement in the Russian Empire received its greatest impetus from Russia's defeat in the war against Japan (in 1905) and from the revolutions in Iran and Turkey (in 1908), the first bourgeois revolutions in the Moslem world. But in Central Asia, there were no revolutionary upheavals until the 1917 socialist revolution in Russia. The major trends of Central Asia's bourgeois development were then taking shape, but the process was interrupted by the dramatic developments in Russia.

Pan-Islamism, pan-Turkism, and nationalism

At the beginning of the twentieth century, two trends became increasingly prominent in Central Asian political life. The first was a growing awareness among the region's peoples that they were united by common interests and a common historical destiny. But the other trend reflected each peoples' desire for self-determination. Ideologies and political movements representing the two trends were divided between two major centres of attraction – religion and ethnocentrism.

The principal ideologies and political movements representing the interests of the Central Asian community were pan-Islamism and pan-Turkism. And the desire for ethnic self-determination was expressed in nationalism. Islam was inseparable from nationalism, but the ideology highlighted the special features of Central Asia's Islam rather than the idea of Moslem unity.

As in all oriental colonies, nationalism in Central Asia was at once anti-imperialist and anti-despotic. It was based on the local people's desire to obtain the same rights as the citsens of Russia and then to transform traditional Central Asian society into bourgeois society.

At the beginning of the twentieth century, the most active political groups in Central Asia were pan-Islamic organisations. In the Russian Empire, such organisations emerged following Russia's defeat in the war against Japan in 1905, under the influence of the growing anti-Russian sentiments in Asia. The common demands of Russia's Moslems were than formulated for the first time. The initiative for setting up a single Moslem organisation belonged to Tatars, who played an important role in spreading pan-Islamism in Central Asia.

The First Moslem Congress was held in Nizhnii Novgorod in August 1905. It adopted the decision to set up a Moslem political organisation, *Itifaq ul-musulmin* (a Moslem Union). The Second Moslem Congress, held in St Petersburg in January 1906, was attended by several hundred delegates representing various regions of Russia, including Kazakh of the Turkestan District. The Third Congress in August 1906 formulated the Moslems' main demands – religious liberty and freedom of education. The Congress also decided to transform the Moslem Union into a political party. The party established contacts with Russia's Constitutional Democracts, but these refused to support the Moslems' demands. The leaders of the first pan-Islamic organisations hoped that the czarist government and the liberal bourgeoisie of Russia would support reforms in the country's Moslem regions, but these hopes were never fulfilled. After a while, the first pan-Islamic organisations ceased to exist, but they were re-established following the revolution of February 1917 in Russia.

There were no regional organisations of Itifaq ul-musulmin in Central Asia. However, pan-Islamism obviously influenced the Jadidists; that influence is seen in the programmes and activities of the first political parties set up by Jadidists. The Jadidists moved from enlightenment to political struggle under the influence of the Young Turks' revolution in 1908.

In 1909, an underground party, the Young Bukharans, was set up by Jadidists of Bukhara. Its first leaders were young merchants and clergymen who had received their education in Turkey. Many of them – Fayzullah Khojaev, Abdul-Kadir Muheddinov, Abdalrauf Fitrat, Akmal Ikramov, and other public figures, writers, philosophers, and publicists – had little to do with Islam.

But an important contribution to the establishment of the party was also made by *ulama*. The leader of Bukhara's Jadidists, who actually founded the Young Bukharans' underground organisation, Mahmud Khoja Behbudi, was a *mullah* of Samarkand; and Miunker Kari (Abdurrashidov) was a pan-Islamist. The party's active members included Qadi Sharifujan, formerly the Supreme Judge of Bukhara, and many other *mullahs* and *ulama*.

Fayzullah Khojaev later wrote of the social base of the Jadidists that supported the Young Bukharans: 'Most Jadidists were medium-income or low-income intellectuals or petty bourgeoisie – religious-school students and minor officials. There were some rich merchants, but, first, they were few, and, second, they were not really active; they mainly provided financial support (Mansurov, Yakubov). We had even high-ranking clergymen – for example, Mullah Ikram (one of Bukhara's 12 *muftis* who sympathised with the Jadidists), the author of a booklet that criticised the emir's government.'[31]

The party's programme centred on three main demands: new methods of teaching, condemnation of obscurantism and religious scholasticism, and resistance to the emir's despotism and Russia's policy in Central Asia.

The Young Bukharans' ideology was aptly described by Benigsen as

Figure 11. Mosque Dolo Khauz, Bukhara

'a curious mixture of Turkish reformism (modelled on that of the Young Turks), Tatar Jadidism, and Pan-Islamism ... extremely revolutionary, anti-Russian and hostile to the emir of Bukhara at the same time'.[32]

The Jadidists of Bukhara published several newspapers – *Bukhara-i sherif* in Tajiki, *Turan* in Uzbek, *Kurshed*, and others. The editorial offices of these newspapers sent a large delegation to Turkey to meet the Young Turks' leaders and established direct contacts with that party. New-method *maktabs* had Turkish teachers, who had close links with the local Jadidists. The Jadidists' political demands published in the press mainly concerned self-government for the Turkestan District and the need to restrict the unlimited powers of czarist officials; they also demanded that a people's parliament (*majlis*) be established in Bukhara to turn the khanate into an enlightened constitutional monarchy. For Central Asia, a region dominated by traditional customs, where the khans' despotism was unrestrained, these were truly revolutionary demands.

During World War I, differences increased between the moderate older enlighteners and the younger Jadidists. The younger Jadidists were led by Fayzullah Khojaev whose supporters were increasingly influenced by communist ideas. But even revolutionary minded Jadidists saw Islam as the basis of their culture and of Central Asian unity. Pan-Islamism, pan-Turkism, and nationalism were closely linked, largely because the development of modern Central Asian nations was not completed by the First World War.

History shows clearly that the major components of ethnoses (the fundamentals of modern languages, the settlement of certain ethnic groups in certain territories, ethnopsychological features, and typical economic structures) began to take shape in Central Asia as long ago as the period between the ninth and the eleventh century and were mostly established by the sixteenth century. Characteristically, Islam had been adopted by tribes that later developed into modern ethnoses by the time the features of those ethnoses had begun to take shape, or was adopted by them in the process. As a result, a strong connection between peoples' religion and ethnic self-awareness, which still exists in Central Asia today, was historically preordained.

Central Asia's annexation to Russia, the construction of railway lines there (which helped to draw its peoples into the sphere of the capitalist market), the process by which nomadic tribes shifted to a settled way of life promoted by Russia's policy and the development of bourgeois relations and enlightenment in the areas incorporated into the Russian Empire, were all factors which undeniably promoted the establishment of modern ethnoses.

Islam and ethnic self-awareness

However, nomadic peoples remained divided into tribes and clans, and local social institutions of permanent-population rural communities and towns remained influenced by traditional tribal relations. According to Central Asian scholars, Central Asian peoples had no concept of Motherland; their awareness of their territories as national entities was dim or non-existent, and parochialism was strong. 'The concept of Motherland', comments M. G. Vakhabov, 'was often limited to people's own town or village.'[33] In that situation, T. S. Saidbaev was right to point out, 'Islam played a certain integrating role in ethnic processes in pre-revolutionary Central Asia.'[34]

The people of Central Asia thought of themselves as Moslems before thinking of their ethnic origin. A mixture of ethnic and religious identity was typical of their social psychology, and that feature remained even throughout the seven decades of the communist regime. Russianisation was never popular in the region in czarist or Soviet times, although the idea was strongly promoted by the Empire's authorities.

At the time of the 1917 socialist revolution in Russia, Central Asia's nationalists had very vague ideas about forms of state independence for the region's peoples, although everyone was eager to gain independence. Pan-Islamic and pan-Turkic ideas were entangled, producing the idea of building a single state to comprise all the Turkic Moslem peoples of Central Asia. It was also proposed that several ethnic states should be established.[35] But representatives of various nations did not have any coordinated programmes. And ideas were vague about the number and the boundaries of ethnic states to be established in Central Asia. Specific programmes for political and cultural division of Central Asia into certain nations, and for self-determination of those nations, were drawn up and implemented in Soviet times. These programmes were produced by the leadership of the Russian Communist Party (Bolsheviks) rather than by Central Asian nationalists.

The integrating function of religion in the development of nations is not specific to Islam, much less to Central Asia's Islam; it is more or less typical of other religions, too, under certain historical conditions. Islam in Central Asia never managed to overcome parochialism or clan and tribal disunity. It acted as an integrating factor consolidating the people of the mainstream religion. But if a nation comprised minority groups professing a different branch of Islam (Shiism), or even a different religion, this led to social and political disintegration. The religion's disintegrating function was especially prominent when religious differences coincided with ethnic ones (as in the Pamirs region and adjacent areas).

Following Central Asia's annexation to Russia, the influence of Islam on the development of ethnic self-awareness increased considerably. Islam was a fully established ideology that could be used by political leaders to unite Central Asian peoples into ethnic entities. So, as they built their first political organisations, they viewed them as parties of co-religionists, united to protect their economic and political interests. A Jadidist newspaper, *Khurshad*, wrote, for instance: 'To ensure the nation's progress, we should boycott merchants of other religions and buy from our co-religionists.'[36]

There is no evidence that Central Asian societies began to be secularised in that period or that Tajik or Uzbek nationalism started to emerge. The first step in that direction was taken by the Jadidists, who opened *maktabs* and secular schools where teaching was conducted in local languages, and published newspapers in those languages. Nationalist ideologies of Central Asian peoples have their roots in the enlightenment of the 1870s–80s. The first works of literature in the languages of major local nationalists were written by religious reformers and enlighteners of that period (and some have been mentioned in this book).

But there were no particular nationalist or political demands formulated by Tajik, Uzbek, or other peoples of Central Asia. The Kazakh people, who were strongly influenced by the Tatars of the Volga River region, were a special case. Kazakh nationalism began to take shape at the beginning of the twentieth century. Its first ideologists developed the ideas advocated by the nineteenth-century Kazakh enlighteners – cooperation with the Russians and opposition to the conservative Islamic forces. In 1912, Kazakh nationalist activists set up Alash-Orda political groups, which served as a basis for a Kazakh political party of the same name, established in March 1917. The party's leaders – Ahmed Baytursinuli (a poet and teacher), Ali Khan Bukei (Bukeikhanov, a writer, folklorist, and historian), and other well-educated Kazakh – were secular people educated at Russian and Tatar schools in Russia and were oriented towards cooperation with Russian democrats from the very outset. They were not Pan-Islamists or Pan-Turkists and advocated the national interests of the Kazakh people.

Another party, Ush Zhuz (The Three Hordes), was founded in the Syr Darya region in 1913. Its founders were *mullahs* of Bukhara and representatives of the local petty bourgeoisie, who had contacts with the Young Bukharans. In contrast with the Alash-Orda of that time, Ush Zhuz had a pan-Islamic, anti-Russian, and anti-Tatar political programme. In 1916, it assumed an extremist position in the struggle for an independent Kazakhstan.

Before World War I, Alash-Orda and Ush Zhuz were the only one-nationality political parties.

The Jadidists and their first political party, the Young Bukharans, comprised people of several nationalities. Ayni wrote, 'The Young Bukharans had members of all the nationalities living in Bukhara – Uzbek, Tajik, Turkomans, Arabs, Iranians, Jews. Tatars . . . marched shoulder to shoulder with us along the path of the revolution.'[37]

Most political leaders of that time spoke on behalf of Central Asia's Moslems, rather than for a certain ethnic group, or on behalf of the Turkic nation, which was then understood to comprise all the Turkic Moslems (Uzbek, Turkomans, and Kazakh). But that did not create ethnic conflicts – largely because the Tajik and other Central Asian peoples had a common religion, Sunnism, which also tended to separate the Tajik from the ethnically close Iranians (who professed Shiism). So, in contrast with many Moslem countries, the Moslems of the Russian Empire knew no conflict between their religious and ethnic self-awareness.

Prior to and during the First World War, Islam not only was the basis of pan-Islamism and a component of nationalism, but also gave rise to holy wars (*jihad*). One example is the uprising of Turkestan's tribes in the Khiva Khanate in 1916.

The Turkoman uprising

In the Turkestan Territory, and in the Turkmenian steppes, the struggle for liberation from Russia was triggered by *ishans*. In 1916, the year of the Turkoman uprising, the entire Turkestan District was engulfed in disturbances. These were triggered by the authorities' decision to mobilise the district's Moslems for service on the home front, which came, worst of all, during the Saum, the Moslem fast. The Moslems' indignation reached a peak in the old Moslem Dzhizak district, where Ishan Nazir Khoja, one of the most respected people there, declared a *jihad* against the Russians. An official government document said, 'It was decided to declare a holy war and move hordes of natives to Dzhizak, to capture it from Russia and establish an independent state there, to be headed by an elected beg.' According to General A. N. Kuropatkin, 'rebellious Moslems' shouted that they did not want to be the Russian czar's subjects any more. The insurgents were led by elected 'people's begs' headed by Ishan Nazir Khoja. The uprising was cruelly suppressed by punitive troops, and the people's begs were hanged.

But that was a serious warning to the czarist government. It became increasingly obvious that Central Asian Moslems could do no more than keep fighting each other or their khans, pinning their best hopes on the intermediary and civilising mission of Russia. There had emerged political leaders who were ready to defend the Moslems' rights under political slogans and even to wage a holy war against Russia. The pan-Islamic opposition was led by educated Moslems, but calls for all-out holy wars against the Russians in Central Asia and in the Caucasus came from *ishans*. Later, when the czarist government was replaced by the Bolshevik Party, the *jihad* in Central Asia was supported by *ulama*, who represented established Islam. But before describing the dramatic developments of those years, let us take a look at the entire period when Moslem Central Asia was part of the Russian Empire. Was the Central Asian Moslems' situation any different from the position of Moslems in other colonies and what were the special features of Central Asia's Islam?

As in other parts of the Orient, the colonisation of Central Asia had mixed consequences. The region's incorporation into the Russian Empire promoted the development of bourgeois relations there, the introduction of modern legislation in the territories directly subordinated to Russian authorities, and the growth of a local intelligentsia, as Central Asia's upper classes obtained access to Russian education. But the people of Central Asia never acquired the same rights as all other Russian citizens and were called 'natives' in all the official documents. For a long time, Russia preserved the influence of the *ulama* on education and judicature – and preserved it to a greater extent than did the colonisers of other oriental countries. The Russian authorities only helped to improve the organisation of established Islam and placed it under their control – thereby separating it from popular Islam, represented by dervishes and *ishans.*

In the khanates, Russia did not interfere in internal affairs, and the positions of *mullahs, ulama,* and *ishans* were not affected by the Russian conquest. Up to the beginning of the twentieth century, Central Asia's religious reformers, enlighteners, and first political leaders actually strove to gain equal rights for the region's people rather than to promote its secession from Russia.

The situation began to change as Russia intensified the colonisation and Russianisation of Central Asia and curtailed the influence of *ulama* on judicature and education there following the suppression of the 1905 revolution. Significantly, the mandate given by the Moslems of Tashkent to their representative in the Second Duma of Russia (convened in 1907), Mullah·Abdulkariev,[38] included the demands to restore *qadi* courts, the election of elders and rural district administrators, and self-government for the Moslem part of Tashkent.

As shown above, a major role in the awakening of political consciousness in Central Asia's Moslems was played by Tatar enlighteners. As modern-style political movements became established in the region, its people became increasingly aware that all the Moslems of the Russian Empire had common interests to promote. Tatar and Bashkir members of the Russian Duma spoke in support of Central Asia's Moslems in 1907. A Bashkir representative highlighted the fact that there were no Kazakh or Kirghiz delegates in the Duma; a Tatar representative of Kazan province issued a warning to the czarist government. For a long time, he said, the population of Turkestan did not realise that it should fight for its rights, 'but now that you deprive people of land, even the people of Turkestan, who have put up with everything until now, may rise in rebellion'.[39] As we know, that prediction came true very soon.

Certain special features of Central Asia's Islam, its synthesis with local pre-Islamic beliefs and tribal traditions, made Central Asian societies stable and steady and difficult to modernise along bourgeois lines. Central Asia awoke to politics later than the other Moslem regions of Russia.

The trading bourgeoisie of Central Asia (industrialists were non-existent in the region) was certainly drawn into the capitalist market.

Nevertheless, in defending their interests, merchants had reasons for continuing to rely on Moslem society and Islam, however reformed it might be.

Because of peculiar features of Central Asia's Islam, *ulama* and *mullahs* were much more active in early national liberation movements there, providing ideological support, than clergymen in many other Moslem countries. But it was also because of these peculiar features that *ishans* and dervishes had more influence with the rural population, and especially with nomads, than official Islam had, and these people remained emphatically hostile to Russia throughout the period of the Russian dominion over Central Asia.

Notes

1. Quotations from the original documents about Central Asia's annexation to Russia are taken from *A History of the Peoples of Uzbekistan*, 1947, vol. 2, pp. 227–53.
2. Translated from *A History of the Peoples of Uzbekistan*, vol. 2, pp. 235–6.
3. S. G. Rybakov, *The Management of the Religious Affairs of Russia's Moslems and Problems Involved Therein* (in Russian), St Petersburg, 1917, pp. 8–10.
4. T. S. Saidbaev, *Islam and Society* (in Russian), Moscow, 1978, p. 111.
5. Ibid., pp. 76–8.
6. A. Benigsen and C. Lemercier-Quelquejay, *Les musulmans oubliés. L'Islam en Union Soviétique*, Paris, 1981, p. 26.
7. N. Dingalstadt, *Judicial Reforms in Turkestan Territory* (in Russian), Moscow, 1892.
8. *Central State Historical Archives of the USSR*, 821, opus 8, vol. 599, list 308.
9. *A History of the Peoples of Uzbekistan*, vol. 2, pp. 235–6.
10. Ibid., p. 262.
11. L. Klimovich, *Islam in Czarist Russia* (in Russian), Moscow, 1936, p. 226.
12. Translated from Saidbaev, *Islam and Society*, p. 112.
13. Martha Brill Olcott, *The Kazakhs*, California, 1987, p. 79.
14. 'Draft regulations for the government of Turkestan Territory, 1903'; 'The consideration of a supplement to Article 270 of the regulations for the government of Turkestan Territory by the Duma and the Council of State', *Colonisation Affairs*, vol. 9, 1911, pp. 251–459; *A History of the Peoples of Uzbekistan*, vol. 2, p. 343.
15. Ibid., pp. 346, 347–54 ff.
16. Ibid., p. 413.
17. A. A. Gordlevsky, *Selected Works*, vol. 3 Moscow, 1962; G. P. Snesarev, *Under Khorezm's Skies* (in Russian), Moscow, 1973, pp. 78–97.
18. B. Yaroshevski, 'The central government and peripheral opposition in Khiva, 1910–1924' in Yacov Ro'i (ed.), *The USSR and the Muslim World*, London, 1984, pp. 16–39.
19. Ibid.
20. Translated from Benigsen and Lemercier-Quelquejay, *Les musulmans*, p. 26.
21. I. I. Velikhanov, *Selected Works* (in Russian), Alma-Ata, 1958, pp. 191–2.
22. The teachings of al-Qursavi, al-Marjani, and Ahmad Donish are thoroughly

analysed in A. M. Bogoutdinov, *Essays on the History of Tajik Philosophy*, Stalinbad, 1961, pp. 241–309. See also S. Ayni, *Materials on the History of the Bukharan Revolution*, Moscow, 1926, pp. 12, 15–16, 25 ff.; *Bukhara Memoirs* (in Russian), vol. 2, 1949, pp. 11, 15 ff.

23. Ahmad Donish, *Extremely Uncommon Events; Risole; A Will*; Y. E. Bertels, 'Manuscripts by Ahmad Qalla', *Transactions of the Tajik Office of the USSR Academy of Sciences* (in Russian), Moscow, vol. 3, 1936.

24. A. Klimovich, *In the Service of Education. The first Turkic-language newspaper Tarjuman and its editor I. Gasprinski* (in Russian) 2, Zvezda Vostoka, 1987.

25. I. Gasprinsky, *The Moslems of Russia* (in Russian), Simferopol, 1881, pp. 3–4.

26. Translated from Gasprinski, *Tarjuman* (in Russian) 2, 1905.

27. Gasprinski, *The Moslems of Russia*, pp. 4 and 7.

28. W. Barthold's letter of 23 September 1913, sent from St Petersburg to N. P. Ostroumov in Tashkent, the Central State Archives of Uzbekistan.

29. Ayni, *Bukhara Memoirs*; P. Mirza-Akhmedova and D. Rashidova, *The Jadidists – Who Are They?*

30. Ibid. See also Benigsen and Lemercier-Quelquejay, *Les musulmans*, p. 42.

31. F. Khojaev, *A Reply to G. Turkestansky*, Tashkent, 1926.

32. Benigsen and Lemercier-Quelquejay, *Les musulmans*, p. 42.

33. *Documents of a Conference Devoted to the Pre-Revolutionary History of Central Asia and Kazakhstan* (in Russian), Tashkent, 1955, pp. 155–6.

34. Saidbaev, *Islam and Society*, p. 82.

35. Serge A. Zenkovski, *Pan-Turkism and Islam in Russia*, Cambridge, Mass., Harvard University Press, 1960; Richard A. Pierce, *Russian Central Asia 1867–1917*, Berkeley and Los Angeles, University of California Press, 1960.

36. Translated from Saidbaev, *Islam and Society*, p. 117.

37. Ayni, *A History of the Bukharan Revolution*.

38. *A History of the Peoples of Uzbekistan*, vol. 2, p. 392.

39. Translated from ibid., p. 396.

CHAPTER THREE

ISLAM AND MOSLEMS OF CENTRAL ASIA UNDER THE COMMUNIST REGIME

The birth of the organised political movement of the Moslems under the impact of the February Revolution in Russia

The February Revolution gave an impetus to the awakening of the national self-awareness of the Moslem peoples. The First All-Russia Congress of Moslems was held in Moscow on 1 to 11 May 1917. It was attended by 900 delegates from all Moslem nationalities inhabiting the Russian Empire, including 300 *malali*. The Volga Tatars and moderate right-wing socialist dominated the Congress. It opted unanimously for the conciliation of Islam with socialism and confirmed the unity of Russia's Moslem peoples. The Congress discussed for the first time the question of the self-determination of the Moslems and their state structure. However, there was no previous unanimity on this question between participants in the Congress. Some advocated the cultural autonomy of the Moslems within a uniform, centralised Russian democratic republic, others called for the territorial autonomy of the Moslems within a Russian federation. The latter scored more votes (446 against 271). The resolution adopted by the Congress said, in part: 'It should be recognised that a democratic republic along the national-territorial-federative lines as a form of the state structure of Russia that best suits the interests of the Moslem peoples is a democratic republic based on national territorial and federative principles with national-cultural autonomy for the peoples that do not have their own territory.'[1]

The Congress set up the Moslem Central Agency, the Moslem Central Council (*Milli Shura*) and the Executive Committee (*Ikomus*).

The Second All-Russia Moslem Congress was held in June 1917. It adopted a decision to organise a Moslem Military Council (Harbi Shura), an All-Russia Moslem Council (*Milli Idora*) and to hold a National Assembly of Moslems in November 1917. As far as state structure was concerned, the Second Congress backed down from the decisions adopted by the First Congress and came out in defence of Moslem democracy, for a broad national-cultural autonomy of the Moslems of inner Russia and Siberia, and for the granting to the

Moslems of the right to decide themselves the question of the form of government in Turkestan, Kirghizia, the Caucasus and Crimea.

The speeches of Second Congress delegates were distinguished by a greater revolutionary spirit and more pronounced pan-Islamic ideas. The Military Council set up by a Congress decision began immediately to recruit soldiers for a Moslem army. However, all these Moslem organisations were not destined to live long, and were disbanded after the October Revolution of 1917 and the establishment of Bolshevik rule in 1918.

The Moslems of Central Asia were not represented at the Congress. They simply could not get there because of the turmoil in Russia at the time. Immediately after the February Revolution, the activities of the political parties Alash-Orda and Young Bukharans formed previously, became more energetic and widespread. At that time Moslem nationalist parties were organised in all big regions of the Russian Empire (such as the Party of Crimean Tatars, *Milli Firqa*, founded in 1917, the Bashkir Party under Zeki Velidi Togana, and the Azerbaijan Party of Turkic nationalists, *Musavat*, founded in 1911). These parties supported limited secularisation and the separation of religion from the state, but deemed it necessary to preserve the Islamic traditions as an inalienable part of their peoples' culture.

Activities of the Alash-Orda

Very serious changes took place in the Kazakh steppes after the February Revolution. The groups belonging to the Alash-Orda took the initiative, establishing their own newspaper *Qazaq*. But there was no unanimity between the groups' leaders. Their activities reflected differences between the Kazakhs of the east and west, north and south. Most leaders connected with the eastern Kazakhs were rallied around their newspaper. After the February Revolution, they convened several conferences of the Alash-Orda.

Officially, the Alash-Orda Party was formed in March 1917, when its programme was adopted. Its main demand was the creation of a Kazakh autonomous area within the bounds of Russia. It was stated in the first paragraph that: 'Russia should be a democratic federative republic', and it was specially mentioned that 'democratic' meant 'popular' and that 'federation' had to be an alliance of small states. Each station entering the federation, the programme said, 'is an autonomy, which is self-governed on the basis of equal rights and interests'. The second conference of the Alash-Orda was the most representative. The resolutions it adopted were a compromise between the pan-Islamists and secular nationalists. The conference recognised the need for placing education under the supervision of the state and the *ulama*, for preserving Islamic courts operating alongside civil ones, and for considering Shariah and the common law of the Kazakhs to be on a par with the civil secular law.

Several delegates to the conference attended the First All-Russia Congress of Moslems. The Kazakh delegates united at the Congress with those from Central Asia, Azerbaijan and Bashkiria. It was the votes of Central Asian, Kazakh and Azerbaijan delegates that decided the question of the territorial autonomy of individual Moslem peoples adopted by the Congress. After the First All-Russia Congress of Moslems and until the defeat of the Kazakhs in the Civil War, the attention of the Alash-Orda leaders was centred around the elaboration of the structure and legal foundation of their state. At the third conference of the Alash-Orda, attempts were made to narrow down Islamic functions in the Kazakh state structure; the sphere of civil law was broadened; the rights of Shariah courts were restricted; and preference was given to secular education. Nevertheless, a considerable number of the Kazakh *Ishans* and *ulama* supported the foundation of a Kazakh autonomous state.

The Provisional Government which, according to its contemporaries, was striving to put an end to anarchy in the Kazakh steppes, recognised the Alash-Orda and agreed to the creation of a Kazakh Autonomous Republic. On 10 December 1917, after the October Revolution in Russia, its formation was officially proclaimed, with two governments – one for eastern and the other for western Kazakhstan. Both governments were headed by the leaders of the Alash-Orda – Dostmohammedov led the western in the village of Zhambeitu, and Bukeikhanov led the eastern in Semipalatinsk.

However, the Kazakhs living in southern Kazakhstan under the leadership of the Tashkent section of the Alash-Orda headed by Togusov, who had never co-operated with Bukeikhanov, did not recognise the Provisional Government. Some scholars believe that these contradictions were connected with Togusov's sympathy for socialism and the sharply anti-communist stand (up to the early 1920s) of Bukeikhanov. Yet Martha Olcot, the author of the most recent detailed work *The Kazakhas*, is apparently right in assuming that the heart of the matter was a power struggle. It is difficult to say anything about ideological differences, especially since, later, Bukeikhanov became a leading national communist.

After the October Revolution in Russia, the first session of the government of the Kazakh Autonomous state was held, in February 1918. Thus, at the very dawn of the revolution, the Kazakhs received definite independence from Russia and a semblance of national statehood. The Alash-Orda Party and the first Kazakh government put forward a demand for the creation of a separate muftiat of the Kazakhs and for the appointment of a special mufti to decide all religious matters of the Kirghiz living in the territory of the Kazakh state.

After the outbreak of the Civil War, the Kazakh supported the White Guard movement headed there by Admiral Kolchak. However, as the latter was completely indifferent to the Kazakhs' national aspirations, their tribal and family traditions and Islam, they preferred the communists, as did many other Central Asian nationalists.

In Turkestan after the February Revolution, the place of the czarist administration was taken by a representative of the Provisional Government. Turkestan's status as Russia's Territory remained unchanged. This caused discontent on the part of the Uzbeks, Tajiks and other Moslem peoples inhabiting the region. The activities of the social democrats and Bolsheviks, as well as of the Union of Working Moslems formed earlier in Tashkent, became more energetic.

The local bourgeoisie and a considerable part of the intelligentsia rallied around the *Shurli-Islamiya* set up previously and which adhered to pan-Islamic positions. The clergy supported the organisation *Ulama.*

Simultaneously with the All-Russian Moslem Congresses, territorial congresses began to be convened in Turkestan. The Second Territorial Moslem Congress discussed the autonomy of Turkestan and a programme and plan for its implementation. Soviets began to be formed on Turkestan's territory. *Mullahs* and *ulama* took an active part in their work. A strained situation developed in the Fergana Valley. In Kokand, its economic and political centre (where there were 382 mosques, 42 *madrasas* and 6,000 Moslem priests) *mullahs*, *ulama* and local nationalists put up a struggle in an attempt to drive out the Russians and revive the Kokand Khanate.

In the Khiva and Bukhara Khanates, the news of the overthrow of the czar was greeted by meetings and demonstrations. The movement for reforms headed by the Jadidists received a new impetus.

In the Khiva Khanate, revolutionary minded and educated young people set up, as did Bukhara's Jadidists, their own organisation of Young Khivans. After the local Russian garrison took an oath of allegiance to the Provisional Government, the Young Khivans handed the Khan a petition for reforms. The Khan entrusted them with the task of compiling a manifesto, published it and appointed a Provisional Committee to supervise its implementation. But it was too early for the reformists to celebrate victory. Although several influential *ulama* of Khiva supported them, the most conservative ones, headed by Mahmud Sharif, came out against reforms, and they

Figure 12. Djuma Mosque (XVIII c.), Kokand

succeeded in setting a considerable number of Moslems against the Young Khivans. Religious, tribal and family ties were still very strong there. After a demonstration of *ulama* with slogans calling for the defence of Islam gathered at the palace, the Khan summoned *malali*, judges, Moslem elders and Young Khivans – that is, the main opponents and supporters of the reforms. The supporters were defeated; the Provisional Committee was disbanded, and many Young Khivans were executed.

In Bukhara, the events took a more tragic turn. A stubborn struggle had been going on for a long time between the Jadidists and Kadimists in the Bukhara Khanate. After the February Revolution in Russia, the Jadidists decided that their hour of triumph had come at last. The Party of Young Bukharans organised 50 cells of 12 people each for work among the broad sections of the Moslems and put four principal demands to the Emir: to create central and provincial systems of people's representatives; to repeal taxes, except those established by the Shariah; to proclaim the freedom of schools and the press, and to replace the most cruel officials. Simultaneously, the Young Bukharans addressed the Provisional Government with a request 'to tell our government to change the way of life on the basis of freedom and equality, so that we might become proud to be under the protection of great and free Russia'.[2]

A delegation of Young Bukharans was sent to Russia. The Provisional Government did not leave their appeal unheeded. It gave appropriate instructions to its representative in Bukhara. On his advice the Emir published a manifesto which satisfied practically all demands of the opposition and removed the Bukhara *Qadi Kolon* Burkhaddin, who headed the group of the most conservative *ulama* opposed to the reforms. But when the Jadidists came into the street in a demonstration with slogans hailing the reform, they were met by a counter-demonstration of *mullahs* and *ulama* under the slogan of the defence of Islam. And most Moslems supported them. The manifesto was virtually withdrawn and the supporters of the reform had to retreat. This prompted the Young Bukharans to seek *rapprochement* with the Bolsheviks and to try to seize power by military means. Immediately after the October Revolution and the establishment of Soviet power in Turkestan, the Young Bukharans set up a Military Committee and sent a delegation to Tashkent asking for military assistance. A Red Guard detachment was despatched to Bukhara. In this way the young Soviet power of Turkestan, according to its representatives, supported 'a revolution which was not popular, which was not connected with the people, which was alien to them'.[3]

The events ended tragically. The Red Guard detachment was defeated and the Emir massacred the Jadidists in Bukhara. More than 3,000 people were killed, among them numerous *mullahs, qadis* and *mudarris* who were members of the Young Bukharans. This massacre dispelled their belief in constitutional monarchy. The Jadidists who stayed alive and managed to preserve their party, according to their own words, 'recognised the idea of Bolshevism as more acceptable'.[4]

The coming of communists to power. Their first steps with regard to Islam. The reaction of Moslem revolutionaries

No matter how we assess the October Revolution in Russia, we cannot but admit that it exerted an enormous revolutionising influence on the colonial east. Of course, that influence differed in different countries and regions. In 1917, the power of the Bolsheviks was established in the Turkestan district only. The remaining Central Asian regions had to be won and the armed struggle for their inclusion in the Soviet state continued until the mid-1920s.

Six stages can be identified in the interrelationships of the Moslems and Soviet power.[5] The first covers the period directly after the October Revolution, when the Bolsheviks were inclined to take into account the influence of Islam, and some of its ideologists even tried to present it as a revolutionary theory which did not contradict the communist idea. The second stage – from 1920 to 1923 – can be considered as the first wave of persecution of Islam and of reprisals against the Moslem clergy. This was connected with the general exacerbation of political struggle and with the attempt of the Bolsheviks to get rid of their most serious rival 'with one sabre blow'. The third stage – from 1923–4 to 1929–30 – saw another search for compromise between the new power and Islam. The prestige of the clergy grew, and their participation in public life became more active.

At the end of the 1930s the epoch of 'the great change' began: the forced construction of socialism started and collectivisation proceeded apace; the political regime lost its last features, if relative, of democracy. A totalitarian system was finally established in the USSR, under which there could be no place for religious views, including those of Islam. This fourth stage, in the 1930s, was perhaps the most difficult for the Moslems: persecution of Islam reached its peak.

The situation changed again on the eve of, and especially during, the Great Patriotic War of 1941–5, that is in the fifth stage, when persecution for religious beliefs and reprisals against the clergy decreased. Moslem priests proclaimed the just character of the war, collected funds and donated huge sums of money for military needs. During the war the Religious Board of Moslems of Central Asia and Kazakhstan was set up. This became the centre and organiser of the Moslem clergy and the mediator in relations between the Moslems and the state. It is interesting to note that, at the time, officials of the Board often occupied the same premises as Soviet administrative bodies, and in some cases even used the same letterheads.

The calm and confident character of the relations between the state and religion continued until the mid–1950s. By that time the aftermath of the war was over, the 'labour enthusiasm' of the population was high enough, and the authorities came to the conclusion that they did not need any support from religion.

Thus began the sixth stage. Religion again became an object of attacks on the part of the higher echelon of the Communist Party. 'Communist education presupposes the liberation of consciousness from religious prejudices and superstitions, which are still preventing some of our Soviet people from fully applying their creative powers,' N. S. Khrushchev said at the 22nd Congress of the Communist Party of the Soviet Union (CPSU). He believed that 'man's intellectual development cannot be successful if his brains are blocked with mysticism, superstitions and false ideas'.[6] The CPSU leadership pointed to the intolerably great number of mosques that were still operating and took measures to close them down. A powerful anti-religious campaign unfolded at the time, which aimed, among other things, to combat religious rites and rituals.

This official policy towards religion, in various forms, continued in subsequent years, and even at the beginning of *perestroika*.

Islam under the Bolsheviks

But let us return to the position of Islam in Central Asia immediately after the Bolsheviks came to power. In an address of the Council of People's Commissars of the Russian Soviet Federated Socialist Republic (RSFSR) (20 November–3 December 1917) to all working Moslems of Russia (the Tatars of the Volga regions and the Crimea, the Kirghiz of Siberia and Turkestan, the Turks and Tatars of the Transcaucasus, the Chechens and mountain-dwellers of the Caucasus) it was said: 'from now on your beliefs and customs, your national and cultural institutions are declared free and inviolable'.[7] A special article of the Constitution of the RSFSR, which was included in the Constitution of the Turkestan Autonomous Soviet Socialist Republic (TASSR), proclaimed freedom of conscience and the right to profess any religion, or not to profess any. Having believed in the first appeals and decrees of Russia, the settled peasants and nomads and many educated Moslems, primarily the Moslem reformers (Jadidists) and some *mullahs*, supported the revolution. Many nationalist parties of the Moslem peoples formed after the February Revolution in Russia entered local branches of the Russian Communist Party.

There had been no communists among the Central Asian Moslems before February 1917. But, during the period between the February Revolution and the end of the Civil War in Turkestan, a local communist organisation had been set up, and several local revolutionaries and activists of the first Central Asian political parties turned to the Russian Communist Party. They began joining it – not individually (like Tatar Moslems), but in whole groups, like the Kazakh Alash-Orda, and the left wing of the Young Bukharans and Young Khivans. They were prompted to do this for many reasons which were aptly outlined by A. Benigsen. They abandoned the White Guard movement primarily because its leaders completely ignored the national aspirations of the Moslems. They were, rather, drawn to Lenin's promises (although these were not clearly formulated), in his April Theses, to grant the Moslems the right to secede from the Russian state, and also to the communists' appeal to the Moslems of the east and to the first decrees of Soviet power. The Moslems still believed naively that the October Revolution on the territory of Central Asia would continue the movement for self-government. Finally, they also believed that communism was the best social system for independent development, which would ultimately enable them to gain the upper hand over the colonialists, including the Russian ones.[8]

As for Marxist-Leninist ideology, they had, as a rule, rather vague notions about it. Sultan Galiev, whom A. Benigsen and C. Lemercier-Quelquejay nicknamed 'the father of the Third World', was the chief ideologist of the local nationalists, who believed that it was socialism that would bring independence to the Moslem peoples of the Russian Empire. From the very beginning, Sultan Galiev strove, first, to create a model of national socialism, taking into account the specific features of Islam, and to bring it to all countries of the Moslem world. Secondly, he strove to liberate the Moslem territories of the former Russian Empire included in the Soviet state from the domination of the Russians.[9]

Sultan Galiev was a supporter of secularisation. In his articles he also recognised the need for conducting anti-religious propaganda in the Moslem regions, but it should be taken into account that, at the time, he could not write otherwise in the open press. Yet, he was against the forced introduction of atheism in Moslem society and advocated the preservation of Islamic cultural traditions, writing, as he did, about the Islamic phenomenon – a special viability of Islam. He suggested that this phenomenon, and the specific features of Islam of each of the Moslem peoples of the Russian Empire (the Tatars, Bashkirs, Kirghiz, Kazakhs, the peoples of Central Asia and the Caucasus), as well as the fact that Islam was a religion of the downtrodden, be taken into consideration. Sultan Galiev warned that the struggle against Islam in Russia would always be taken as a missionary activity, as an attempt to spread another religion, alien to the people, and to perpetuate Russian domination.[10]

However, the communist authorities did not heed Sultan Galiev's voice. Moreover, he himself fell victim to Stalin's reprisals. But his ideas proved prophetic to a certain extent. His views about national socialism became widespread in eastern countries in the 1950s–70s. The forced introduction of atheism failed to eliminate Islam; it only compressed it like a spring, which immediately straightened itself as soon as the communist regime collapsed. Sultan Galiev's calls for the independence of Moslem peoples inspire many nationalists even today, and his forecasts concerning the viability of Islam were confirmed by the Moslem movement in the former USSR in the late 1980s and early 1990s.

There were outstanding representatives of national communism among Central Asian revolutionaries. They were, above all, the leaders and ideologists of the Young Bukharans, Abdalrauf Fitrat and Fayzullah Khojaev, the Kazakh nationalists – the creators of the Alash-Orda Party, Ali Khan Bukei, and others.

Central Asian national communists

All Central Asian national communists proceeded in their revolutionary theory from a number of general premisses. They regarded the Moslem nations as proletarian, and consequently the class struggle there should be stopped until they won complete independence from Russia, since the October Revolution did not automatically abolish the functions of Russia as a colonial power. All national communists continued to distrust the colonialist nations, be they European or Russo-Eurasian. They maintained that a socialist revolution should begin in the Moslem regions of Russia, primarily in Central Asia, with a national liberation revolution, which should be headed by the national communists without Russia's help.

As for Islam, the Central Asian national communists, like Sultan Galiev, believed that it should be secularised, but that its great cultural heritage should be protected and that Moslem civilisation should be saved from the colonisation by Russian and other European powers.[11]

All Central Asian national communists suffered the tragic fate of Sultan Galiev: in the late 1930s they were executed as the 'enemies of the people'.

It is important today to recall that far from all the Central Asian revolutionaries preserved their illusions with regard to communism and the communist regime. In 1919, the local socialists in Tashkent decided to organise their own National Socialist Party, ERK (Will). An independent decision on the formation of a National Socialist Party was also adopted in Bashkiria. In November 1919, the socialists of Tashkent, Bukhara, and Bashkiria, adopted a decision to join their efforts in creating such a party. At a congress of the peoples of the east in Baku, in September 1920, an organising commission of the new party was set up. It had become clear by that time that the Central Committee of the Communist Party of Russia would not tolerate the existence of a legal socialist party. The centre of the new party's activity was transferred to the Bukhara People's Republic created at the time. At the First Congress of the Socialists of Central Asia held in Bukhara in April 1921, which was attended also by representatives of the Kazakh and Khiva republics, the creation of the Turkestan Socialist Party (Tude) was proclaimed. The Congress also adopted a programme for the Party. Turkestan's position within Russia was described as the position of a colonial country 'under the domination of one of the imperialist powers'. The Tude called for economic and political independence. 'The form of government in Turkestan, freed from the imperialist yoke from without and the domination of the feudal lords and clergy from within, should be a democratic republic.'[12]

At the same time, the Party called for the preservation of national cultural traditions. However, in contrast with the national communists, the socialists did not stress the specific features of Islam and confined themselves to a general demand from all secular parties for separation of the church from the state and for the complete freedom of conscience.

After the communist regime put an end to the independence of the first popular republics of Central Asia – the Bukhara and Khiva republics, the Tude Party went underground. In the late 1920s some of its leaders emigrated; the rest were executed, just like national-communists in the late 1930s. Although after the October Revolution Soviet power displayed caution towards Islam, in contrast with its attitude towards other cults, it had already taken, in 1918–20, the first steps along the road of forced secularisation. The officially proclaimed inviolability of religious beliefs and customs had already been frequently violated during the first stage. Following the Decree on the separation of the church from the state, and of the school from the church, in 1918, the teaching of the fundamentals of Islam was banned, not only at state-run and public schools, but even at private educational establishments and mosques. Marriage and divorce according to the Shariah had no legal force. The *mullahs* and *ulama* were regarded as representatives of the exploitative classes and deprived of electoral rights, and their rights to jobs were restricted.

Simultaneously, Soviet power launched an onslaught against the *qadi* courts that had existed in Central Asia for centuries. A 'resolution on the local courts of *qadis* and beys' envisaged their reorganisation and replacement by a uniform people's court. It was recommended that 'the new courts accept only those foundations of the Shariah which did not contradict the legal consciousness and conscience of the proletariat'.[13]

The government of Turkestan, meanwhile, decided simply to abolish Shariah courts in August 1919. The first measures adopted by the Council of Ministers of the Turkestan Territory were in flagrant contradiction with Bolshevik promises to protect the rights of Moslems. Turkestan government officials effected the separation of the church from the state and the school, and of the courts from the church, in absolute disregard of the specific features of Islam. Such a ruthless attack on Islam in no way corresponded with the fact that, at that time, faithful Moslems, provided they were workers, peasants, or in general belonged to the poorer sections of the population, could be accepted in the Communist Party or even represented in the bodies of power. Akmal Ikramov, Secretary of the Central Committee of the Communist Party (Bolsheviks) of Uzbekistan, later recalled that during the Third Congress of Soviets of Turkestan in 1918 many delegates left the conference hall to conduct prayers.[14]

In these circumstances there could be no talk of any consistent line towards Islam. More far-sighted and better-educated leaders and theorists of the Russian Communist Party (Bolsheviks) recommended that the specific features of Islam in Central Asia be taken into consideration at the first stage; others simply ignored them. The local authorities heeded now the former, now the latter, depending on who stood nearer to whom. Meanwhile, each measure restricting the activities of the clergy and encroaching on the traditional Islamic institutions and the religious rights of the Moslems, only added fuel to the flames of the Basmachi movement which had began in 1917 and had engulfed the greater part of Central Asia by 1920.

The truth about the Basmachi movement

The communists called 'Basmachi' ('robbers' in Uzbek) those who declared war on them immediately after their coming to power in Central Asia. That war, which continued unchecked until the mid-1920s, came to be known as the Basmachi Movement, a term which defined it as an anti-popular war. This definition of the movement has firmly entrenched itself in the consciousness of Soviet people and in Soviet literature. Western Kremlinologists, of course, threw it into doubt at once, but they did not have enough information to disclose its true nature.

After the beginning of *perestroika*, much new data from the archives appeared in the Soviet press. It was high time to tell the truth about the Basmachi Movement corroborated by facts.

The Moslem *ulama* and *ishans* were the first to declare war on the communists who came to power in Russia and established their domination in Turkestan. With the exception of the most enlightened

Figure 13. Madrasa Kulkeltash (XVI c.), Tashkent

representatives of the Moslem clergy, they always distrusted and, more
often than not, displayed open animosity to, Russian domination. They
hated the new power even more than that of the czar. It was not simply
the power of foreigners and adherents of a different faith; it was the
power of atheists.

When the Bolsheviks came to power in Tashkent, the situation in
Turkestan was troubled and unstable. The struggle for the autonomy
of the territory, which began under the Provisional Government, did
not cease. The first measures of the Council of People's Commissars of
the Turkestan District in Tashkent only poured oil on the flames.

In November 1917, the Extraordinary Congress of the Moslems of
Turkestan proclaimed the independence of Turkestan and elected its
government. Turkestan thereby found itself divided into two parts –
one Soviet with its centre in Tashkent and headed by the Communist
Soviet (or Council) of People's Commissars, and the other the Moslem
Turkestan with its centre in Kokand and the government of *ulama*,
local nobility, and representatives of the bourgeoisie. That was the
actual beginning of a civil war. In December 1917, on the birthday of
Prophet Muhammad, demonstrations took place in support of the
Kokand government in all big cities of Turkestan. On the night of 30

January 1918, Soviet units launched an offensive on Kokand and took it by storm on 5 February, killing all its defenders. That was how communist power reacted to the first Moslem attempt to put an end to colonial dependence.

The Moslem *ulama* of Fergana raised the banner of *jihad*. It was not only the fighters for religion that gathered under this banner, but all discontented Moslems, whose number was growing with the introduction of the food surplus-appropriation system in Turkestan. Numerous Turkoman tribes supported town- and country-dwellers.

After the capture of Kokand and the abolition of autonomous Turkestan, the authorities began to persecute harshly representatives of Fergana's clergy. Speaking at a meeting of the Turkoman Executive Committee, one of its members, Atabayev, admitted that 'our units attacked mosques and threw bombs at praying *ulama* and *ishans*. As a results, all *ulama* and *ishans* went over to the Basmachi.' Atabayev defined the anti-Soviet movement in Turkestan in the following way: 'In 1919–20 it was not armed banditry or the Basmachi movement that operated in Fergana, but a genuine popular uprising.'[15] There is nothing to be added to this.

In the critical situation which had developed in Fergana, the Central Committee of the Russian Communist Party appointed leaders there who were better acquainted with the local conditions. With the help of concessions made to believers they succeeded in splitting the *ulama*. This was also facilitated by the reorganisation of the Red Army and a great effectiveness of military operations against the Basmachis. Khoja Mat Ishan, who was greatly revered in Fergana as a saint, the spiritual leader of the Basmachis, ended his struggle against Soviet authorities. However, this did not stabilise the situation. The villages supporting the Basmachis were destroyed by the Red Army, while the villages recognising Soviet power were razed to the ground by the Basmachis. Then the *ulama* began to call on believers to make *hijra* (departure from *dar ul-harb*, the country of the enemy) to a country of Islam, and *hajj* (pilgrimage) to Mecca.

Individuals, groups and sometimes whole villages began to sell their homes and chattels and to leave their native parts. Fergana was threatened with the prospect of becoming depopulated. Then the Central Committee of the Russian Communist Party appointed a special commission headed by Frunze to fight the Basmachis. The communists again had to admit that it was not the military resistance of the Basmachi units that was invincible; it was the adherence of the Central Asian peoples to Islam, its spiritual leaders and social institutions, that could not be conquered.

The *ishans, mullahs* and *ulama* raised high, in other parts of Central Asia, the banner of a sacred war which had been unfurled in Fergana.

According to eyewitness accounts, they were supported by local residents everywhere. The leaders of Basmachi units received the title *Amir al-Muslimin* (the ruler of the faithful). The *imams* read sermons supporting the *jihad* in the mosques, which remained almost the only centres of public life.

The events in Bukhara gave a new impetus to the Basmachi Movement. These events were known in Soviet historiography as the 'Bukhara revolution' for quite a long time, whereas in Western literature the term 'revolution' has never been applied to them. They were referred to as a coup prepared in advance by the communists with the help of the Young Bukharans, the overthrow of the Emir and the occupation of Bukhara by Red Army units. Arguments are still going on in the Soviet press on the subject. However, new archive documents increasingly show that Soviet Russia annexed the Bukhara Khanate in September 1920. These developments were presented by the command of the Turkestan Front as 'revolutionary fraternal assistance to the people of Bukhara', as help to the Young Bukharans. History repeats itself. Those events in the past resemble strikingly the pattern of the Soviet troops' invasion of Afghanistan in 1979.

Figure 14. Old Muslim cemetery, Bukhara

Of course, one could hardly deny the presence of a revolutionary ferment in Bukhara after the October Revolution. We have attempted earlier to describe the historical fate of the Jadidists and their party of the Young Bukharans. The Jadidists were indeed opposed to the despotic rule of the Emir of Bukhara, but before the October Revolution they were only dreaming of a constitutional monarchy and the complete independence of their khanate. The idea of the overthrow of the Emir was given to them by the Bolsheviks and, as the events of 1918 showed, it was not supported by the people of Bukhara. Nevertheless, on the eve of the 1920 events, it had several advocates in Bukhara. The idea of revolution was supported by the extremists among the Young Bukharans, the Bukhara Communists Party, organised with the direct assistance of the Russian Communist Party (Bolsheviks), by the Command of the Turkestan Front and many members of the Revolutionary Council of Turkestan. Their views did not always coincide with Lenin's recommendation and that of some other members of the Central Committee of the Russian Communist Party on this question. For instance, Lenin wrote in 1918 about the possibility of exporting revolution to Bukhara: 'What could we do for such people as the Kirghiz, Uzbeks, Tajiks and Turkomans, who up to now find themselves under the influence of their *mullahs*? Can we approach these people and say to them: "We shall overthrow your exploiters". No, we cannot do this because they are completely subordinated to their *mullahs*.'[16]

The command of the Turkestan Front called the Bukhara question 'the most accursed problem'.[17] When the Emir made an attempt to improve relations with communist Russia and sent a mission to Moscow, the Chairman of the Central Committee of the Bukhara Communist Party, fearing a favourable outcome of the mission, sent a telegram to Frunze: 'Circumstances changed sharply calling for immediate action'.[18] Units of the Red Army began to be deployed in Kagan. On 2 July, the buildings belonging to the government of Bukhara were seized, including the Emir's palace; the guard was driven away, and an enquiry of Bukhara's foreign minister remained unanswered. The Bukhara *mullahs* demanded that the Emir order that arms be distributed among the people to defend Islam from the unfaithful. On 7 July 1920, the Emir signed a decree on *jihad*. The command of the Turkestan Front also prepared for military operations. They only waited for instructions from Moscow. However, its political course towards the Central Asian khanates was not clearly elaborated. Nevertheless, a directive of the Politburo of the Russian Communist Party Central Committee was sent to Tashkent on 11 August 1920, to say that 'the replacement of defensive measures by an onslaught on our initiative can only take place provided there is a more or less popular Bukhara revolutionary centre (on our territory, at least), calling on us to start such an offensive.' But there was no such centre in Bukhara. It should be set up urgently. It was decided at the Fourth Conference of the Bukhara Communist Party on 18 August to unite Bukhara communists with Young Bukharans, and on 25 August, the 'Party Centre for Leading the Popular Revolution in Bukhara' was formed. It included V. Kuibyshev, N. Huseinov and V. Khojaev, who issued an order on the same day 'to start active operations at dawn on 29 August in order to render revolutionary fraternal assistance to the Bukhara people'.[19]

On 27 August, the Young Bukharans captured Stary Chardzou and set up a revolutionary committee. The offensive of the main units of the Red Army began, according to the order, on 29 August, and on 2 September Staraya Bukhara was stormed and seized. The Emir fled to the east of the country and the All-Bukhara Revolutionary Committee took power, proclaiming the creation of an independent Bukhara People's Soviet Republic. The government formed by the Committee consisted predominantly of Young Bukharans, their average age being 29. The 'independence' of the Bukhara Republic was protected by the units of the Red Army deployed in Bukhara. The Republic was unable to organise an army of its own. The new power did not enjoy the trust of the population and it was destined to last only 1,420 days, that is, exactly the time required by the Russian Communist Party (Bolsheviks) and the command of the Turkestan Front to crush the Basmachi Movement.

In 1920, the Khiva People's Socialist Republic was formed, which also existed for only a few years.

Immediately after the occupation of Staraya Bukhara by Soviet troops, the Basmachi Movement engulfed the entire eastern and southern parts of the Bukhara Khanate. The Emir, who had fled from his capital, entrenched himself in Gorny Badakhshan and continued the *jihad*. He gathered an army of 15,000 men. A Soviet military expedition dispersed his troops, and he himself fled to Afghanistan. But, according to despatches of the Political Department of the Bukhara grouping of the Turkestan Front, the Emir's army was not destroyed; it became 'scattered in villages, but could be gathered together at any minute'.[20]

The Basmachi Movement on the territory of the former Bukhara Khanate did not end until the mid-1920s. In 1922, an especially difficult situation developed in the south of what is now Uzbekistan, where the forces of the nomad tribes of Lokaya and Turkmen, the nationalists of Kokand and Bashkiria, as well as units of Enver-Pasha (one of the leaders of the Young Turks who fled from Turkey in 1918 and joined the Basmachis) united with the detachments led by *mullahs* and *ishans* under the banner of *jihad*.

The situation in Turkestan proper was also turbulent. In April 1922, Moslem religious and nationalist leaders illegally held a Moslem Turkestan Congress in Samarkand, which adopted a manifesto proclaiming the formation of a Turkestan–Turkic independent republic and recognising the main demands of the leaders of the Basmachi Movement: the preservation of private property and the restoration of Shariah laws.[21]

It became increasingly clear that military force alone would not crush the Basmachi Movement. What was needed was a well-thought-out policy on the land question with regard to the nomads, and, what is most important in a Moslem country, concessions to Islam.

Forced concessions to Islam and transition to forcible introduction of atheism

The Decree of the Central Committee of the Russian Communist Party (Bolsheviks) of 18 May 1922 'On Turkestan–Bukhara Affairs' pointed to the need to change the policy towards the Moslem clergy and Moslem social institutions. It also envisaged the return to their former owners of the lands which used to belong to the clergy, the restoration of the *qadi* courts, and the legalisation of *madrasas* and other religious schools. This decree was implemented. In the Bukhara and Khiva republics, which existed from 1920 until 1924, and in Turkestan (TASSR), the *malali* and *ulama* received all civil rights, the land was returned to the clergy and the *madrasas* and *qadi* courts were legalised. The constitutions of the Bukhara and Khiva republics did not contain the provision for separating the church from the state. Friday was declared a day of rest. A Religious Board was set up in Tashkent, for the first time in the territory's history.

Representatives of the clergy began to be admitted to the local bodies of government. But all of this was a forced concession; 'inasmuch as these men are still influencing popular masses, who do not follow us as yet, I think that until we win over these masses to our side, we shall not have to rub them out', a Communist Party figure wrote at the time.[22] *Mullahs* were even admitted to the Communist Party. In 1923, believers constituted 65.5 per cent of the Bukhara Communist Party and 44 per cent of the Turkestan Communist Party. Only Russian communists were predominantly atheist in these parts. There were 200 *mullahs* among the members of the Bukhara Communist Party, according to the official statistics of 1924. However, numerous *mullahs* who were members of local Soviets and were even considered communists, sympathised with the Basmachis and frequently helped them. We have recorded of a speech by Mullah Sharif, Chairman of one of the local revolutionary committees, and Mullah Sali-ogly, member of the committee, who were sent to villages in 1925 to conduct an anti-Basmachi propaganda campaign. They were not afraid to admit to local Moslems that they did this under pressure from the Russians.[23]

Sometimes, however, *mullahs* and *ulama* did indeed render assistance to the Soviet authorities in the 1920s. When, in 1925, the Central Asian Bureau of the Central Committee of the Russian Communist Party (Bolsheviks) adopted a decision on the confiscation of beys' land, cattle and agricultural implements and distributed them among peasants, devout Moslems refused to take them, for the Shariah forbad them to acquire the property of others. Then Mullah Abdul Hafiz Mahdum, Chairman of the Tashkent Religious Board, issued a special appeal to believers, explaining why the use of beys' land by the peasants should not be prohibited. Referring to the Koran, he proved that land belongs to those who 'revived' it, that is, to those who till it with their own labour. He cited passages from the Koran telling how the followers of the Prophet gave their favourite gardens and other possessions to the poor. Consequently, the appeal said, the beys should themselves give away their lands, and if they do not do this, the government has the right to confiscate them and to distribute them among the peasants. Of course, Mullah Mahdum was appointed to his post by the Soviet authorities. Nevertheless, his appeal had an effect, especially since it was backed up by similar appeals to believers issued by many other *imams*.

Inconsistency of communist attitude

Yet, the Soviet authorities constantly antagonised even those *mullahs* who sympathised with them by pursuing their policy. Under the threat of the continuing Basmachi operations, and being vitally interested in cooperation with *ulama* and *ishans* who had such a great influence on the Moslems, the communists' attitude and behaviour were extremely inconsistent. This was most vividly expressed in the situation with Shariah courts. In January 1920, the Central Executive Committee of the Soviet Turkestan Republic adopted a decision on the formation of a 'commission for coordinating laws and orders of the workers' and peasants' government of the Turkestan Republic'. The commission's duty was to see to it that, in case of differences between the Soviet laws of the Republic and the laws of the Shariah, the former laws should be revised at the People's Commissariat of Justice and changed accordingly.

In July 1922, the Turkestan Central Executive Committee, on a recommendation of the Congress of Legal Workers, issued a decree on restoring the activities of the Shariah courts of *qadis*. These courts were not financed by the state budget, but existed on remuneration from the cost of court proceedings (they received a certain percentage of civil actions' costs). A similar situation, as we remember, prevailed in czarist times. But hardly had six months passed since the adoption of this decree of the Central Executive Committee, when the law on Shariah courts began to be revised. They were allowed to operate in three regions only – Fergana, Samarkand and Syr Darya, that is where the Basmachi Movement was especially strong. By 1924 all criminal cases had been withdrawn from these courts. Only in the Bukhara People's Socialist Republic did the courts of *qadis* retain their rights as long as the Republic existed, that is until 1924. All in all, there was 65 *qadi* districts in the Republic. All *qadis* were employed by the state, and five of them were members of the Bukhara Communist Party.[24]

Despite the constant narrowing down of the Shariah courts' functions, they enjoyed great prestige in the rest of Central Asian territory, too, even after its territorial demarcation; in 1925, there were 86 *qadi* districts in Uzbekistan alone.

After the inclusion of the entire territory of Central Asia in the USSR in 1925, the attitude towards Islam of the Russian Communist Party and, consequently, of the local bodies of power, was again distinguished by growing negative trends. A letter of instructions issued by the People's Commissariat of Justice to the chairmen of regional courts and regional prosecutors provides an indication of a new attack on the traditional institutions of Islam. It said, in part: 'You should, jointly with party committees and public organisations, and not later than 28 October, ascertain and report to the People's Commissariat of Justice the opinion of the working masses in the districts where the *qadi* courts still exist, in order to assist a decision by the government of the Uzbek Soviet Socialist Republic, which would correspond to the wishes of workers and peasants, by the tenth anniversary of the October Revolution.'[25] That was how the Soviet tradition of doing away with Islamic institutions (in this case, the *qadi* courts), 'by the will of the working people' and for a memorable date, came into being.

The policy towards Moslem education was also inconsistent in the first half of the 1920s. There were cases of *mullahs* being persecuted for teaching the fundamentals of Islam in mosques, though sometimes permission was given to teach Islam in Soviet schools. Conditions were more favourable in the Bukhara and Khiva republics. However, there, too, religious schools were gradually ousted by Soviet schools, the essential difference between them being an official permission to teach faith and to pray and, on completion of the first grade, to study Islam at mosques. After the abolition of these peoples' republics, these permissions to study religion were automatically withdrawn.

All-out attack under Stalin

When the all-out attack of socialism on all spheres of life began in the USSR in 1929, the Stalinist regime switched to the forcible introduction of atheism in Central Asian society. The beginning of the campaign was marked by a decree of the All-Russia Central Executive Committee of the RSFSR of 8 April 1929, 'On Religious Associations'. The believers' rights, freedom of conscience, consideration of religious traditions, painstaking explanatory work – all was declared on paper only. Between 1928 and 1938 the local communist parties were purged of all Moslem nationalist leaders without exception. Some were exterminated as 'nationalists' and Islamists, others as 'sultangalists' (supporters of Sultan Galiev), pan-Turkists, 'spies' and 'traitors'. The All-Russia Military Committee of Moslems and the All-Russia Moslem Council had been banned in 1918, and now their leaders, who lived on Russian territory, were murdered. *Ulama, mullahs* and sheikhs were purged and most of them exterminated. Their activities were banned. Moslem fraternities (*tariqas*) were declared illegal. The land belonging to religious institutions, which supported religious schools, was nationalised. Mosques were closed and destroyed, and *madrasas* could no longer function legally.[26]

However, this enormous layer of traditional religious and cultural life did not disappear altogether; it went underground. Adherence to Islamic traditions remained, but the number of traditionally educated people dwindled. Most representatives of educated *ulama* and *mullahs* of the older generation died in forced labour camps, while young priests were unable to receive traditional education. Islam continued to be propagandised, but it was done now by uneducated, ignorant *mullah*, much more fanatical than their predecessors.

The hardest blow to the culture of the Moslem peoples of the former USSR was dealt by the forced transfer of their written languages from the Arabic alphabet to the Cyrillic alphabet. The cultural tradition, of which Islam was an inalienable part, was thus broken. Islam was deprived of its place in the state structure, but the struggle to restore its place in society and the state persisted.

The adaptation of the Moslems of Central Asia to the communists regime

Did a well-thought-out policy towards Islam of the Communist Party of the Soviet Union and the Soviet government take shape after the formation of the USSR? Facts show that it did not. The general policy of forced introduction of atheism and suppression of freethinking did not take into account the specific features of Islam. Nevertheless, there were general guidelines with regard to the the Moslems of Central Asia and the desire of the authorities to penetrate into Moslem social structures.

As pan-Islamism and calls for the unity of the Turkic peoples were the slogans of the liberation struggle against Soviet domination in Central Asia, the main priority was to abolish the idea of the common interests of the Moslems, the traditional affinity of the Turkic-language peoples and the community of the historical destinies of the Turkic-language and Iranian-language peoples of Central Asia. This aim was served by the territorial demarcation of Central Asia, which began in 1924 and ended in 1939, and also by the policy of pursuing the artificial separation of Islamic traditions from national ones, and by the deliberate opposition of secular nationalism, which had already taken shape among individual peoples of Central Asia, to Islam and pan-Islamism.

Prior to the territorial demarcation of Central Asia, its main lands were part of Russia, having acquired the status of autonomous republics: the Turkestan (with the greater part of Uzbek and Tajik territories), Turkmen and Kirghiz. (It should be remembered that, in view of the complicated process of ethnogeny, the Kazakhs in czarist Russia and in the first years of Soviet power were called Kirghiz. Soviet power was established on their territory in 1920.) The Bukhara and Khiva People's Republics, formally independent from Russia (which included mainly Uzbek, Tajik and Turkmen lands) existed, as we have seen, for only four years (from 1920 to 1924). The territorial demarcation of Central Asia divided lands between three Union republics: the Uzbek (which included the Tajik Autonomous Soviet Socialist Republic), the Turkmen and the RSFSR. The Russian Federation also included the former Kirghiz Autonomous Republic, which was later renamed the Kazakh Autonomous Soviet Socialist Republic, and the separate autonomous region of the Kirghiz (which was called at first the Kara-Kirghiz, and from 1926, the Kirghiz Autonomous Region). The status of a Union Soviet Socialist Republic was given to Tajikistan in 1929, and in 1936 to Kirghizia and Kazakhstan. The territory of the south of Kazakhstan (Semirechensk and Syr Darya regions) where its capital, Alma-Ata, is situated, lies in Central Asia.[27]

The instability of the administrative borders of Central Asia derived from the interests of the centre, the difficulties which it encountered in the forced stimulation of the transition from nomadic to a settled ways of life, and the rivalry of the traditional and newly formed local party élites. Administrative frontiers did not correspond to the settlement of the main nations. Besides it was very difficult to draw a demarcation line on ethnic principles. Not a single newly formed administration was ethnically homogeneous, and there were disputed territories in each of them (Bukhara and Samarkand in Uzbekistan for instance), which created constant hotbeds of ethnic tension.

It can hardly be denied that the changes occurring after the inclusion of Central Asia in the USSR contributed to the formation and development of local ethnoses and to the growth of nationalism. Industrialisation, the expansion of cities, the emergence of the local national intelligentsia, with the help of the Soviet centre and the Russian intelligentsia – all this led to the creation of secular political culture and national self-awareness. But all these processes were taking place at an élitist level. The mass of the population remained Moslem in their consciousness and way of life. The very term 'Moslem' denoted, first and foremost, the people's belonging to a definite regional culture, but not the degree of their religiousness. Representatives of the new intelligentsia, striving for self-identification and for the self-determination of their ethnos subconsciously, and quite often consciously (as far as it was allowed by the communist regime), did not distinguish national traditions from the Islamic sources, and representatives of each nation wanted to prove that their culture was more ancient than that of their neighbour.

The Tajiks have long considered themselves the genuine keepers of Islamic traditions in Central Asia, because their ancestors adopted Islam earlier than did the Turkic-language ethnoses.

The Islamic influence on the political culture of individual ethnoses was not simple. The most essential differences existed between the ethnoses whose nucleus was formed by the settled population, and those who had recently been nomads. This was reflected in the role played by Islam in the social structures and political culture of the regime, and especially after the disintegration of the USSR. Official Islam's prestige, as we understand it, was very high among the Uzbeks, and especially the Tajiks; it was not so high among the Kazakhs, Kirghiz and Turkmen. Islam was less dogmatic there. The *ishans* and their disciples (each of them had sometimes 500 pupils and followers), who constituted an inalienable part of the local social structures, had more influence on the population than the *ulama* in the years of Soviet power. During that period, Islamic institutions were closely intertwined with family and tribal ones amid former nomads. They were distinguished by considerable stability, and numerous customs and rites were observed legally, even during the forced introduction of atheism, because they were regarded as national traditions rather than religious ones.

Crushing of Islamic structures

The local authorities during the 1930s wished not only to crush the Islamic structures, but also to penetrate and subordinate them. For example, in Kazakhstan (especially in its southern, Central Asian part) the local authorities, in their struggle against the influence of the Sufis, often orientated themselves towards official Islam and supported the Kazakh *ulama* in their desire to separate themselves from the Central Religious Board of Moslems of inner Russia and Siberia and to set up Moslem boards.

Under the communists' regime, it led to the destruction of the former hierarchic structure of guidance of the Moslem community in Kazakhstan: *mutavaliat* and *muhasabat* (Religious Board and All-Russia Congress of Moslems). In the late 1930s, the *mutavaliats* and *muhasabats* were destroyed on Kazakhstan territory.

As for the *ishans,* they were almost completely exterminated. The Vaisis were brutally persecuted in all republics of the former USSR. In 1917, Inan Vaisov, the son and successor of the founder of the sect, Bahaaddin Vaisov, supported the Bolsheviks, received arms from them and was killed in battle fighting on their side in February 1918. Nevertheless, his fraternity was subsequently banned by the Soviet authorities. His followers had a tragic fate, as did other local nationalists and priests who supported the revolution and Soviet power in its first years.

Nevertheless, despite the abolition of a number of the Moslems' spiritual institutions and the physical extermination of a greater part of the clergy, certain social structures synthesising Islamic and local clan traditions were preserved in Central Asia, although the very foundations of the existence of these institutions seemed to have been undermined. There was no legal opportunity to follow the Shariah, and there was no place to study and propagandise Islam. These difficulties notwithstanding, Islam did not simply survive under the communist regime: it demonstrated its creative potential, having preserved to this day such traditional social structures in Tajikistan and Uzbekistan as the *makhallas.*

'*Makhalla*' is a Tajik word meaning 'a part of town or village', which represents a traditional Central Asian community adapted to modern

Figure 15. Tombstone Ibn Abbas (XIV c.), Mosque Shah-i Zinda, Samarkand

life. It remains the basic cell of the social structure of Central Asia to this day. Each *makhalla* always had a mosque, but from the late 1920s to the early 1980s this had operated clandestinely for it was not officially registered. After the Second World War, the policy of the forced introduction of atheism became less pronounced. Religious Boards were restored and some mosques, which had not been destroyed, were officially registered. However, until the 1980s there were very few such registered mosques. In Tajikistan they comprise less than one per cent of all operating mosques. The *imams* of the registered mosques were appointed by the local authorities. However, they belonged, as before, to hereditary *ulama* families, who were regarded as descendants of Muhammad or of local saints. The *mullahs* and *ulama* recognised by the authorities and holding official posts, represented, and still represent, official Islam.

The *makhalla* is headed by an elected committee of *aksakals* (the Elders). Each Moslem who has reached the age of 40 is considered *aksakal*. He represents his family in the *makhalla* and is responsible for the behaviour of its members. The *aksakal* is viewed by the *makhalla* as the keeper of the national traditions closely connected with Islam. The most respected *khanum* supervises the behaviour of women, their observance of family traditions and the proper education of children. The latter learn the customs of Islam and are brought up within the family. When they begin studying at a secular school, they are already conscious of being Moslems. The secularisation of education and society as a whole and the introduction of atheism were unable to destroy this traditional structure and its religious and clan connections.[28]

The communist authorities were forced to recognise the *makhalla* and made every effort to incorporate its leadership into the Soviet structure of power and to subordinate it to themselves. They could remove the *aksakal* or *mullah* who did not wish to cooperate with them, but they were unable to destroy the traditional Islamic way of life. The secular intelligentsia, which came into being in the years of Soviet power, but which could not free itself completely from the influence of Moslem traditions, was also unable to do it.

The Sufi orders *tariqas* constituted an inalienable part of unofficial underground Islam after the mass reprisals of the communist regime against the clergy began. The activity of the sheikhs was, as before, connected with Moslem sacred places – a tomb, a tree, etc. Official Islam was against the activity of the *tariqas*. However, many of its representatives were closely connected with sheikhs, or were sheikhs themselves. This became evident in social and political life only when the reforms of the 1980s started in the former USSR.

The open penetration of the CPSU leadership in the centre, and in the provinces, into the official structures of Islam started after the outbreak of the Great Patriotic War of the USSR against Nazi Germany. During the war the Soviet government again agreed to legalise official Islam. In 1943, the Religious Board of Moslems of Central Asia and Kazakhstan was formed, with its headquarters in Tashkent. At first it showed independence and began to collect donations for *uraza* from the believers, in accordance with the rules of Islam, and in 1945 it issued a *fatwa* declaring these donations obligatory. However, the Board's activity was subordinated to the law on religious cults, and this *fatwa* became virtually invalid.

Pilgrimage to Mecca was officially allowed in 1944. In 1945 the Miri Arab *madrasa* in Bukhara was reopened, and the Imam Ismail al-Bukhari Mosque in Tashkent resumed operations. A Religious Academy was organised in Tashkent under the Board. The best students began to be sent to Moslem universities abroad, primarily to al-Azhar in Egypt. To control Moslem institutions and take part in their work, the CPSU began to send communists of Moslem nationalities to al-Azhar.

The Religious Board was allowed to have publications. In 1946 it began to publish in Uzbek (written in Arabic script) a quarterly

Journal of the Religious Board of Moslems of Central Asia and Kazakhstan,
which was replaced in 1969 by a magazine entitled *Moslems of the Soviet
East* published in Uzbek, and, since 1947, in English and French.
However, the number of copies was negligible and they were
accessible only to the clergy and party élite and were meant mainly for
foreign readers.

Mufti Babakhanov's book *Moslems of the Soviet Union* was printed in
rather small numbers. In an interview with a French magazine in
1980, the author noted that there were 100 big, and more than 500
ordinary, mosques in Uzbekistan alone which were visited on Fridays
by up to three million believers.[29] The number of mosques was, by
itself, insignificant, but their functioning in the conditions of the
communist regime and the number of people praying in them were
eloquent enough.

Theory of the modernisation of Islam

Following the example of individual *ulama* of al-Azhar, who were
elaborating the concept of 'Islamic socialism' under President Nasser,
Central Asian *ulama* put forward their own theory on the
modernisation of Islam. Its main premises were outlined in the
above-mentioned Moslem publications, *fatwas* issued from time to
time by *muftis*, in Friday sermons by the *imam-khatibs* of big mosques,
in reports at conferences organised by the Board under the direct
control of the CPSU, and in radio addresses by *muftis*. The essence of
these concepts preached by the *ulama* of the Central Asian republics
(just as in other Moslem regions of the USSR, for that matter) can be
summarised thus: (1) Islam is a religion corresponding to the
prevailing conditions of the modern world in the greatest measure;
(2) Islam is the least dogmatic and most dynamic religion of all; (3)
Islam is a harbinger of socialism and contains its main principles; (4)
Islam is the religion of the oppressed and unfortunate; (5) Islam is the
only religion capable of preserving human morals and values from the
destructive influence of modern technocratic civilisation; (6) Islam
contains the spiritual sources of the national culture of each people of
Central Asia; (7) Islam is the most internationalist of all religions.
There is nothing original in this interpretation, and it has much in
common with the ideas of many other reformers of the Orient in the
latter half of the twentieth century.

After the war, the CPSU leadership began to encourage the
international activity of the *ulama* in every way. Delegations of *ulama*
went to Moslem countries in Asia, and they received delegations of

Moslems from abroad. *Ulama* representatives participated in all regional, republican and All-Union conferences of peace supporters, were members of local peace committees and of the All-Union Soviet Peace Committee. The Central Asian Moslem organisations took part in the conference of all churches in Zagorsk in 1952, in the Asian Conference for Lessening Tension in International Relations in New Delhi in 1955, and so on.

In the 1960s, the CPSU leadership, while preserving the outwardly legal status of official Islam and the Islamic spiritual institutions created under USSR government supervision, again resumed a policy of forced introduction of atheism. However, the foreign political activity of the Board, under government control, was naturally encouraged.

Effect of the Afghan war

The Soviet aggression in Afghanistan (1979) and the Islamic revolution in Iran (1979) posed a serious threat to the foreign political ties of Central Asian official Islam and to its prestige among the Moslems of their own country and of the entire Moslem world. The Moslems of Central Asia, and first and foremost of Tajikistan, largely sympathised with the Afghan *mujahidin* and Khomeini.

It is common knowledge that some young Tajiks, actually quite a few of them, took part in the anti-Soviet movement in northern Afghanistan, with its centre in Kanduz. The movement's leader, Azad beg, was a relative of the famous Basmachi leader in Central Asia during the 1920s, Ibrahim beg, so his popularity with the Tajik Moslems was naturally great. From the mid-1980s onwards, soldiers of Central Asian nationalities began to be replaced with representatives of other nationalities of Russia. According to eyewitness accounts, soldiers from Central Asia started revealing religious solidarity with the *mujahidin*.

In these circumstances, representatives of official Islam found it exceedingly difficult to justify the Afghan war. It was especially difficult to do so since the entire Moslem world, with the exception of a few countries of the so-called socialist orientation, denounced the invasion of Afghanistan by Soviet troops. The Soviet government made desperate attempts to improve the situation, particularly by stepping up the foreign political activity of the higher echelon of Central Asian *ulama*. From 1970 to 1980, seven international Moslem congresses and conferences were held in Tashkent, Samarkand and Dushanbe. However, in view of the fact that Moslem countries did not respond to the Board's invitation, the conference in Dushanbe was attended, apart from delegates from the countries of socialist orientation and Turkey (who had been present at all previous international meetings), by representatives from Saudi Arabi, Jordan and North Yemen. An international conference organised by the Board in Tashkent in 1980 and devoted to the beginning of the fifteenth century of the era of *hijra* did not produce the desired result. The most influential countries of the Arab world, Indonesia and the African Moslem countries refused to accept Mufti Babakhanov's proposal. A major reason for this was the fact that the Board's dependence on the communist regime was becoming ever more difficult to conceal from foreigners. Babakhanov's speech at the international conference in Tashkent in 1980 repeated, word for word, the basic premisses of the CPSU with regard to the Afghan war, US imperialism, and so on.

It is interesting to note that information about the position of Islam in official party documents in Central Asia republics, and in atheist literature printed in the centre and provinces, influenced the evaluation of Western scholars. They have written some very important works about the position of Islam in the Russian Empire and in the republics of the former USSR. Among them are works by A. Benigsen, C. Lemercier-Quelquejay, Steckelberg, Trimingham and others. They cite important information about adherence to Islam in Soviet Central Asia and justly note that the forced introduction of atheism could not deprive the believer of the opportunity to fulfil the basic requirements of Islam: *ash-shahad* (preaching monotheism and recognising the prophetic mission of Muhammad), *as-salat* (prayer), *as-saum* (fast), *az-zakat* (tax for the poor). The only exception was *al-hajj* (pilgrimage) – the Soviet Moslems received permission to make it only after the Second World War.

Because there is much information about how Soviet Moslems observed Moslem religious rites during the years of Soviet power, we shall not dwell on this at length in this book. It is noteworthy that, while citing all these interesting facts, Western scholars maintained, back in the 1970s, that 'Islam in particular no longer influences Central Asian society as an all-embracing social movement equally involved with politics, law and collective morality. It now operates almost exclusively at the individual level'. Islam 'never possessed a strong, unified institutional structure', and 'for these and many other reasons', it 'has found itself singularly ill-equipped to meet the challenge of new ways and new ideas'.[30]

This conclusion was made by Keith Scott in the early 1970s, when he submitted his work to the collection *Soviet Central Asia. A Religious Limbo. Religions and Societies. Asia and Middle East.* As the collection came off the press in 1982, its editor deemed it necessary to make a special reservation saying that the events of the late 1970s disproved some of the assessments made by the author, and that the turn of political events in Central Asian republics would show whether or not he was right in his main conclusion. As we now know, the author's forecast and that of his fellow thinkers was not correct.

Central Asia did not stand apart from the so-called Islamic upsurge which enveloped many countries of the Moslem world in the 1970s. Adherence to Islam began to be more evident in these republics' political life, despite the claims of the local authorities that the influence of religion was constantly diminishing.

Underground Islam

From the end of the 1960s underground Islam became noticeably more active. In Kazakhstan and Kirghizia the clandestine activities of the Sufis continued throughout the entire Soviet period. In Tajikistan and Uzbekistan, they received a fresh impetus after the revolution in Iran. Underground mosques were set up along with *madrasas,* and the activity of the Sufis was stepped up.

In 1969, the government of Uzbekistan adopted a special law (not published in the press) 'on the need to intensify control over the

Figure 16. Mausoleum al-Astuna, Termez

observance of the legislation on the questions of religion', which gave special instructions to stop the activities of the *ishans* and pilgrimages to sacred places, to prosecute for propaganda of the Koran and other religious literature, to ban the activities of unregistered, roaming *mullahs,* etc. Serious efforts were undertaken to use *muftis* in the struggle against the Sufis. However, the attempts to abolish traditional ties between the clergy and Central Asian orders, which came out as the keepers of popular Islam by orders from above, failed. True, several decrees were issued denouncing, in a rather mild manner, worship of sacred places, but they did not denounce the *ishans* themselves, despite pressure from the authorities.

It should be said that the *ishans* and underground *mullahs* did not oppose representatives of official Islam, despite the latter's co-operation with the Soviet authorities.

The almost 70-year domination of the communist regime in Central Asia was unable to shatter the traditional Islamic structures, which had existed there for centuries.

Now, to sum up and make general observations.

In the earlier chapters, we drew readers' attention to the fact that the Moslem peoples inhabiting the territory of the former USSR, notably Central Asia, had followed various historical routes. These distinctions are connected with the specific feature of each national culture, language differences, and the peculiarities of economic structures. (We should remind the reader that most Moslems in Central Asia belong to the Turkic ethnic group, which is, in a sense, opposed by the Tajiks who belong to the Iranian group.)

All this, in the final analysis, conditioned the specific development of each particular Moslem people after the October Revolution of 1917. At the same time, under totalitarian rule, the Moslem peoples developed common or similar behavioural and psychological stereotypes. On the one hand, there were attempts to preserve 'pre-socialist' stereotypes, and on the other there was the desire to adapt themselves to the changes connected with the attempts to establish a new social regime. A certain 'opposition ferment' was emerging within Moslem society, which allowed the believers to protect the traditional ways and save their Islamic mode of life.

Reasons for the self-preservation of Islam

What are the reasons for the self-preservation of Islam in the conditions of a harsh totalitarian regime? First, communist ideology proclaimed ideas which were formally in line with the egalitarian notions of Islam. The point is the priority of collectivist values over individual ones and the evaluation of the social and purely human significance of the individual being based on his service to the community.

Hence, a special role was allotted, in these two ideological systems, to communal and state ownership of land, its riches and water. Indicative in this respect is the often repeated reference, in theological and religious-political works, to the well-known premiss which says that 'people together possess the three – water, pasture and fire', which was a sort of endorsement of the nationalisation of the public wealth and its transformation in absolute state property.

There is a certain parallelism in the political premisses of Islam and communism. In both there is an idea of firm power personified in a strong political leader pretending to the role of the ideological (spiritual) head. The communists did not have to 'train' the Moslems to charisma. Simply, a change of concrete political symbols gradually took place.

The fact that the traditional ties of an openly paternalistic character, which were modified and acquired a new 'Soviet' hue but did not change their essence, were not destroyed in the course of the socialist transformations in the Moslem regions of the USSR, was of particular importance.

The 'harmony' of communism with Islam within the limits of the USSR has now been noted by certain Russian economists, sociologists and historians. For instance, this theme is present in works by the Moscow scholar S. P. Polyakov, who adduces an effective and convincing scheme of how Soviet political and economic institutions merged with traditional ones, creating intricate, paradoxical structures. In these structures, lands of the clergy were untouched, forming part of *kilkhoz* land tenure, the *makhalla* council, which often acted as a 'Soviet of people's deputies', retained its influence, and each *makhalla* had its own 'unofficial' clergy .[31]

All this makes it possible to conclude that there was an organic connection, from the point of view of the local tradition between social principles, economic standards and laws, and the mode of government which was established on Moslem lands after 1917.

It should be noted, however, that despite a vividly pronounced egalitarian tendency in Islam and the stable priority of the collectivist spirit, the Moslem religion has never been an insurmountable obstacle standing in the way of the emergence of bourgeois relations in the economy. It was only the fact of making egalitarian ideas absolute, which was a consequence of community spirit plus communism, and plus totalitarianism as a political system, that raised an insurmountable barrier to a market economy and political liberalism.

Along with the above-mentioned objective factors, several subjective ones were also at work. Among these was the Bolsheviks' fear of the Moslem peoples they did not know, whom they nevertheless planned to use as 'fuel' to fan the flames of a world revolution. It is known that Vladimir Lenin, the leader of the Bolsheviks, called on his followers to be more attentive to 'the peoples of the East . . . For our entire Weltpolitik,' he wrote to Zinovyev, who had been sent to Turkestan, 'it is very, very important to win the trust of the indigenous population . . . to prove that we are not imperialists . . . This is a matter of world importance. We must be exceptionally strict and cautious. Otherwise it will tell on India, on the Orient. It's no joke. We must be one thousand per cent cautious.'[32] Suffice it to recall that the well-known Bolshevik military commander, Mikhail Frunze, sent to Turkestan from Moscow to establish Soviet power there, knew oriental languages and was familiar with the Koran. One of his first decrees declared Friday a holiday.

Finally, one other factor hampered the struggle against Islam. The point is that the Extraordinary Commission (Cheka) and its later modifications – the People's Commissariat of Internal Affairs (NKVD), the Ministry of State Security (MGB) and the State Security Committee (KGB) – because of the geographical remoteness of many Moslem settlements and the climatic conditions in Central Asia, were unable to establish absolute control over the life of Moslems. The system of informers was comparatively weak and in general proved ineffective in the context of firm family and clan ties.

At the same time, the stability of traditional Moslem society and its capacity for self-regulation under Soviet power, did not at all mean that Islam and communism coexisted peacefully over that period of more than 70 years. On the contrary, they were both carrying on a struggle, now open, now 'clandestine', for the right to preserve or force a way of life on man. Islam emerged victorious in that struggle.

The dual political policy towards Islam, remained, with certain modifications, throughout the entire period of Soviet power, and even at the start of *perestroika*.

Characterising the attitude of the CPSU towards Islam, Guldz-hakhon Bobosadykova, Secretary of the Central Committee of the Communist Party of Tajikistan, who later dealt with the introduction of atheism throughout the entire Soviet Union, identified it with class struggle and emphasised that 'our class enemies are still lending a religious tint to ideological subversion'.[33]

Public criticism of Islam practised by higher party functionaries and their entourage was accompanied by protection of the collaborators from among the clergy. Reports sent to Moscow about the successes scored in atheistic work were, as it was noted, fictitious. This was known by the local officials who compiled them, as well as by the party ideologues and administrators in Moscow who read them. Atheistic work was unable to undermine the roots of Islam as a mode of life.

Besides, an overwhelming majority of the indigenous population of Central Asia was engaged in the traditional economic sector, in trade, and also in the domain of services. The modern industrial sector created during the years of Soviet power employed mainly people of Slav origin who had come to Moslem lands comparatively recently. The Europeanised intelligentsia proved to be a very small group and its influence on society was quite limited.

Finally, the milieu of party and government officials was actually a consistent champion of the traditional system of social relations sanctified by Islam. Having protested their atheism, numerous important officials, after retirement, proclaimed their adherence to Islam and publicly demonstrated their religiousness.

It is known that educated *mullahs* could reach the higher clerical spheres only with the approval of the secular administration. However, there have been quite frequent instances of an official wishing to mount the administrative ladder appealing for help to the Elders and Moslem dignitaries.

In short, Islam was a natural regulator of socio-political life, although it was not always seen or felt on the surface. And this fact had always to be taken into consideration by all state and political figures.

In a totalitarian society, official Islam and secular state and political structures proved to be so closely intertwined that they could scarcely be penetrated by any members of the opposition.

We have already spoken about Islam as a uniform socio-cultural and political complex existing in time and space. However, one should bear in mind that there are two levels in Islam whose relationship determines the open character of one or another Moslem nation, its readiness to absorb the achievements of other regional civilisations, and its ability to develop its own spiritual and cultural heritage.

From this point of view, the Soviet Islamic province has found itself in a comparatively more difficult situation than Islam in the Middle East, for example.

Isolation of Soviet Moslems

It is known that, on the eve of the 1917 Revolution, despite the general socio-economic and cultural stagnation of traditional society in the Russian east, primarily in Turkestan, the region was also distinguished by the development of the trends common to the entire Moslem world. We have in mind, first of all, Moslem enlightenment and reformist trends coming from abroad. But in the neighbouring countries, enlightenment and reforms formed the basis for a breakthrough of the Moslem peoples, in the latter quarter of this century, to relatively high economic and cultural levels; on the other hand, this was necessary for their self-assertion as a great civilisation with an as yet undisclosed creative and heuristic potential. Soviet Moslems, as we have noted in preceding chapters, were in many ways isolated from these enlightenment and reformist ideas. The process of the revival of religion, and of trying to find the purport of the fundamentals of Moslem civilisation, was violated in this country. This has led to a general stagnation in Moslem thinking and, consequently, in social thought and culture, for these two are indissolubly linked in Moslem society.

Special mention should be made of the Sufi fraternities connected with popular Islam, which, having formally turned away from public life, actually influenced it. These fraternities, as organised religious centres, caused anxiety in the administration, which feared any organisation not approved by them. The Sufi fraternities actually opposed the secular authorities, for they continued to exert an enormous influence on the consciousness and way of thinking of the Moslem population, above all on those who had recently been nomads. More often than not, their authority was so high that their influence within the administrative system even surpassed that of government officials.

There were cases of fraternities deciding the question of the appointment of government officials, interfering in the distribution of municipal housing and controlling work of provincial bazaars. There was an amusing incident when, on the demand of the leader of the regional organisation of a fraternity, a group of passengers was taken aboard an airplane without tickets.

So Islam, contrary to the dual nature of its position and persecution, has remained, as before, the guardian of spirituality and the protector of a collective conscience, and a regulator of relations between people.

This is why the sudden emergence of Islam on the political scene seemed to be a natural phenomenon. The renaissance of 'Soviet Islam' was a direct consequence of the processes which were interrupted in the 1920s and 1930s, or continued in a latent form.

Notes

1. Information about political parties and congresses of the Moslems of the Russian Empire during the period between the February and October Revolutions in Russia is cited from documents of Moslem political parties 1917–20, *Programmes of the Moslem Political Parties*, Society of Central Asian Studies, Reprint Series no. 2, Oxford, 1985, pp. 11–12 ff. Information about the national liberation movement of the Kazakhs is cited from Martha Brill Olcott, *The Kazakhs*, California, 1987, 130–42 ff.
2. Cited in F. Kazymov and B. Ergashev, 'The Road was chosen by the Kurultay', *Rodina*, 1989, no. 10, p. 33.
3. A. Y. Galperin, *Events in Bukhara. New Turkestan*, 9 April 1918.
4. Ibid.
5. An attempt at such periodisation in Russian science was undertaken by T. S. Saidbaev, *Islam and Society.*
6. 'Proceedings of the 22nd Congress of the CPSU', *Gospolitizdat*, Moscow, 1961, pp. 111, 112, 193.
7. 'Decrees of Soviet power', *Gospolitizdat*, vol. 1, 1957, pp. 39–40.
8. A. Benigsen and C. Lemercier-Quelquejay, *Les musulman*, pp. 58–9, 63, 64.
9. Sultan Galiev, 'Methods of anti-religious propaganda among the Moslems', *Zhizn natsionalnostei*, December 1921; A. V. Sagadiev, 'Mirsat Sultan Galiev and ideology of the National Liberation Movement', *Analytical Review*, 1990; Benigsen and Lemercier-Quelquejay, *Sultan Galiev. Le père de la révolution tiers mondiste. Les inconnus de l'histoire*, Paris, Fayard, 1970.
10. A. V. Sagadiev, *Sultan Galiev and Ideology of the National Liberation Movement*; Benigsen and Lemercier-Quelquejay, *Sultan Galiev.*
11. Benigsen and Lemercier-Quelquejay, *Les musulmans,* pp. 63–4.
12. *Programmes of the Moslim Political Parties*, pp. 110, 123.
13. Muslim Bureau of the Russian Communist Party in Turkestan, Tashkent, Turkgosizdat, 1922, p. 23.
14. A. Vishnevsky, 'On the policy of the Communists of Turkestan and Bokhara towards Religion', *Nauka i religiya*, no. 2, 1990, p. 52.
15. Records of the 5th Session of the Fourth Plenum of the Turkestan Central Executive Committee on 5 July in Tashkent. These and other material were taken from *Otkryty Arkhiv* and Yuri Paporov, 'The white sun of the desert', *Unost*, pp. 80–5.
16. V. I. Lenin, *Collected Works*, vol. 38, p. 138.
17. These and other archive materials about Bukhara developments in 1920 are taken from F. Kazymov and B. Ergashev, *The Bukhara Revolution* and 'The road was chosen by the kurultay'. A. Krushelnitsky, 'Dictatorship by telephone', *Rodina*, no. 10, 1989, pp. 31–9; see also R. Shukurov, *Bukhara*, September 1920; 'Necessity of new vision', *Izvestia Akademii Nauk Tajikskoi SSR*, Series Vostokovedenya, Istoria, Philosofia, no. 4 (20), 1989, pp. 75–6.
18. Cited in *Rodina*, 1989, no. 10, p. 34.
19. 'Directives of the command of the front of the Red Army', *Collection of Documents*, Moscow, vol. 3, 1976, p. 550.
20. Cited in *Rodina*, no. 10, p. 37.
21. Saidbaev, *Islam and Society*, p. 139.
22. Vishnevsky, 'How it was done in Central Asia. On the policy of the Communists of Turkestan and Bukhara towards religion', *Nauka i religiya*, no. 2, 1990, p. 51.
23. Ibid.

24. 'Second collection of valid laws and decress of the Bukhara People's Government, Bukhara, 1923', *Turkestanskaya Pravda*, no. 162, 10 August 1923, pp. 17–19.

25. Vishnevsky, 'How it was done in Central Asia', *Nauka i religiya*, no. 2, 1990, p. 53.

26. 'Letter of instruction sent by the Kazakh Territorial Committee of the All-Union Communist Party (Bolsheviks) to all party organisations of the republic on measures to intensify atheist propagands not later than 15 September 1928'; 'Resolution of the Kazakh Territorial Committee of the All-Union Communist Party (Bolsheviks) on the realisation of a decree of the All-Union Central Executive Committee on closing down and banning religious schools', 21 April 1929, and other documents in the collection *Overcoming the Religious Influence of Islam*, Alma-Ata, 1990, pp. 171, 192 ff.

27. USSR Academy of Sciences to the Republics of Central Asia, 1924–34, Moscow-Leningrad, 1934. A. Agzamkhojaev, *The Soviet Multinational State*, Tashkent, 1962.

28. S. P. Polyakov, *Traditionalism in Modern Central Asian Society*, Moscow, 1989.

29. Benigsen and Lemercier-Quelquejay, *Les musulmans*, p. 198.

30. Keith Scott in Carlo Caldorola (ed.), *Soviet Central Asia. A Religious Limbo. Religions and Societies. Asian and Middle East*, Monton, Berlin, 1982, p. 253.

31. Polyakov, *Traditionalism in Modern Central Asian Society*. See also 'Central Asia: Islamic Factor?', *Analytical Review*, no. 6, Postfactum Information Agency, April 1991, pp. 14–16.

32. Lenin, *Collected Works*, vol. 53, p. 190.

33. *Questions of Scientific Atheism*, no. 31, p. 193.

CHAPTER FOUR

THE FIRST STEPS OF ISLAMIC RENAISSANCE

The *perestroika* which began in the Soviet Union in 1985 was rather unexpected for Central Asia, for its ruling élite and for the overwhelming majority of the local population. The ideas of *glasnost* and democratisation which came into being in Moscow and Leningrad (now St Petersburg again) at the time were little understood by, and often absolutely alien to, the inhabitants of Tashkent and Dushanbe, Ashkhabad and Bishkek, to say nothing of village people. At a time when freethinking was becoming widespread in the centre of Russia, the Baltic republics and in Caucasus, very few people dared to raise their voices against the local authorities in Central Asia. The Central Asian party bosses were paying lip-service to the new policy, but in actual fact they cursed it.

Only part of the local intelligentsia, both westernised in the Russo-Soviet manner, and traditional, who stubbornly adhered to national and religious traditions, looked with hope towards the waves of transformations, unthinkable previously, which were surging from the Kremlin.

Like Moscow dissidents, Uzbeks, Tajiks and Kazakhs, sitting in their primitive kitchens or courtyards under dusty plane trees, talked endlessly about Gorbachev, *perestroika,* and the changes in Moscow, and cursed on the sly their own leaders who were doing their utmost to prevent the winds of change from reaching Central Asia. But those were intellectuals; the broad masses of people had no clear idea about what was going on in Moscow.

As before, the faithful attended meetings held by local cells of the Communist Party, took part in socialist emulation, prayed in 'official' mosques, performed clandestinely Moslem rites and rituals, and asked merciful Allah to grant them a better lot.

In those strange years, the editor-in-chief of the influential Egyptian journal *Manar al-Islam* wrote that *perestroika* was nothing but a result of the action of the divine forces, because 'given all the abilities of man and the gigantic possibilities of modern technology, no one could predict the vast reformist cataclysms which shattered the enormous world around the capital of communism – Moscow. The reason lies in the extremely limited character of human abilities as compared with the possibilities of Heaven about which it is said in the Koran: 'He will command, if he so wishes, and tell him "Be!" and so it will. Such is the force of the Almighty.'[1] And who knows, maybe he was right.

The attitude of Moslem enlighteners in Daghestan (an autonomous republic of Russia on the west coast of the Caspian Sea, just opposite Central Asia) was quite in line with the words of the Egyptian journalist. In the first issue of the newspaper *Islamskiye Novosti* (Islamic News) published in Makhachkala, the capital of Daghestan, its editor-in-chief, Maksud Gadzhiyev, explained the essence of Gorbachev's transformations in the following way: 'In April 1985 [the beginning of *perestroika* in the USSR] the tireless prayers of the believers and the moans of the innocently perished were at long last heard by the Almighty who granted us liberation from the "evil spirit"... Perestroika became indeed a sign of Allah.'[2]

Such was the train of reasoning of an 'average statistical' Moslem in the USSR who relied more on the will of God (or the authority of the powers that be?) than on his own view on political questions. His feelings and political mood were dominated by stubborn fatalism born of Islam and consolidated by decades of the almost complete absence of rights under Soviet power. This 'average statistical' Moslem was sometimes completely indifferent as to who decided his fate – Allah or a big party boss. A great paradox of the Soviet system which 'descended' on Islamic soil lay in a whimsical mixture in human consciousness of traditional values and communist tenets, in the intertwining of the communist or socialist with the national and religious.

This explains why political scientists, historians and religious scholars studying the position of Islam in the Soviet Union have been interested in whether they should consider 'Soviet Mohammedanism' as an inimitable social cultural phenomenon, as an integral part of the communist system, or in whether they should regard Soviet Islam as, above all, a remnant of a great regional civilisation which, by the will of tragic fate, fell under the domination of Bolshevism. In other words, should they speak about Islam in the context of communism, or about communism which broke into traditional Islamic society?

The view of the authors of this book is as follows: Islam, despite reprisals and persecutions, has managed to preserve its main features. Considerable changes in the economy and the political structure of Central Asian society (part of which was Europeanised, or 'Sovietised') notwithstanding, Islam as a mode of life has retained its influence on the way Soviet Moslems conceive of the world and develop their moral and political ideas.

Comparing Islam's position with that of Orthodoxy, it becomes evident that Eastern Christian religion suffered much greater losses in the years of communist rule and found itself virtually defeated, while Islam managed to preserve – openly or implicitly – its influence at all levels of social being.

The beginning of Islamic renaissance is connected with the growth of nationalistic tendencies on the one hand, and, on the other, with the slow comprehension (also of a nationalist tint) by part of the intelligentsia of their belonging to Moslem civilisation. This was reflected in the revival of the traditions of Islamic enlightenment which seemed to have been lost forever.

It is in Central Asia (and to a lesser extent in the North Caucasus, except Daghestan) that this trend manifested itself most vividly. The movement of enlightenment proved viable enough, despite all difficulties and losses, and its participants continue to be active even today.

Main aim of Moslem enlighteners

The main aim of Moslem enlighteners has been the revival of classical Moslem culture, familiarisation of Moslems with history, the philosophy of religion, the improvement of morals, etc. It could justly be said that these Moslem enlighteners, in different conditions and at a higher level, were the continuers of the traditions of underground schools and clandestine circles and groups for the study of the Koran and Sunna, which existed before *perestroika*. On the other hand, these people could be regarded as the followers of the great tradition of Islamic enlightenment which emerged in the Middle East late last century and became widespread in the Russian Empire. Thus, during the 1980s a kind of reconstruction of one of the general processes that emerged and developed in the Moslem world at the end of last century and in the first quarter of this century, took place in the Moslem regions of the USSR.

Besides, enlightenment continued the 'traditions of the Moslem Jadidists who had done so much for the modernisation of traditional Moslem society in the Russian Empire and were so mercilessly crushed by the Bolsheviks.

Among modern enlighteners are representatives of different sections of society. There are students of the humanities, journalists, young Moslem priests, simply those who think they know the Koran, the fundamentals of the Shariah and the history of Islam better than others. For example, Dzhabor Saidov, a resident of the Tashkent district of Chilansor, told one of the authors of this book how he studied the Koran all his life, trying to comprehend its essence, familiarised himself with the life of the Prophet, and never hoped to be able to share his knowledge with others. Once, after the beginning of *perestroika,* his neighbours came to see him and asked him to tell them about the life of the Prophet and what the Koran says about justice. He began to tell them about all this sitting on his garden bench. Soon it transpired that his neighbour's brother could write a little in Arabic. Thus a kind of '*makhalla* school of Islam' came into being. At first the authorities were rather suspicious of it. But then, when they saw that there was no harm done to anything or anyone, they even allowed them to use school premises.

This simple story is very typical of Uzbekistan, and of other republics which were recently Soviet and are now independent Moslem states. The story we tell here refers to 1988 when the number of such schools was growing rapidly. There are no statistical data on this subject, but one can be sure that such circles, groups and schools were organised in practically each city district in 1987–90.

Most of these devotees of cultural-religious enlightenment were selfless, unambitious politically and religiously tolerant people. As a rule, all enlighteners of today are young, although there are several over the age of 40. There are people who began to engage in this activity illegally, being subjected to persecution by the authorities.

At these clandestine meetings and gatherings, participants, first in a whisper and later openly, denounced the communists, declaring them responsible for all the sufferings and misfortunes which befell the Moslem peoples – and not only Moslem, for that matter. Those who were fighting for Islam before *perestroika* were especially active. Among them in Uzbekistan were the supporters of Imam Rakhmatulla. In Tajikistan, Wahhabites began to step up their activity in such cities as Kurgan-Tyube, Kulyab and Dushanbe; and the first groups of Moslem enlighteners appeared in the south of Kazakhstan and in Kirghizia, mainly in the Osh Region bordering on Uzbekistan.

Two points should be borne in mind in this connection. First, the greater religious activity and increase of Moslem enlightenment work in Central Asia were preceded by the first steps towards the revival of the Russian Orthodox Church. The late 1980s were marked by an unusual upsurge of Orthodoxy, which began again to claim the role of spiritual leader. Soviet power, in the person of its head, Mikhail Gorbachev, apologised to the Orthodox believers and clergy and began to renounce the direct supervision of church affairs. Hundreds of churches were turned over to parishioners, and cathedrals that lay in ruins began to be restored. Priests appeared on television screens almost every day, discussing matters of religion, Orthodox, of course.

Some priests turned political figures, attempting to connect the will of God with the idea of democratic *perestroika*.

All this provokes a question among Moslems, primarily among the Moslem intelligentsia and clergy: why is it allowed only to Christians? Are Moslems and Islam less important?

Secondly, Islamic renaissance began not only in Central Asia, but also in large cities of Russia. We have in mind the greater activity of Moscow and Kazan Tatar Moslems, who, using political liberalisation, began to form groups to study the Koran, Shariah, history, Islam, and even their own native language, which many of them, living in the Russian environment had begun to forget. The revival of Islam in the centre of Russia exerted influence on subsequent events in Central Asia. The very fact that the Moscow authorities do not any longer oppose Islam has lent additional strength to the Moslems of Central Asia.

Finally, Islamic renaissance in Central Asia did not have one single centre. It began, and went on taking place, in several republics simultaneously. This helps to confirm that the process had long been ripe within traditional Moslem society.

The struggle for the return to the Moslems of mosques which the Soviet authorities had been using for economic and administrative purposes for decades, was one of the elements of this process. The same was true of Russian Orthodox churches. However, it should be noted that sometimes the use of mosques for these purposes was very insulting for believers. For instance, a mosque in the Uzbek city of Chimkent was used as a sobering-up centre. And in one of Tajik cities, the municipal authorities wanted to turn a mosque into a public lavatory. The famous Guboz Mosque in the Uzbek town of Namangan was converted into a storehouse for vodka and wine.

Incidentally, it was around this mosque that one of the first big clashes between the authorities and believers took place. It showed that the former were no longer able to ignore the demands of the latter. A group of active supporters of Imam Rakhmatulla demanded that the mosque be turned over to the town's Moslem community. The authorities not only refused to talk to the Moslems, but also arrested the ringleaders. They threatened to start a hunger strike. People began gathering around the mosque. The impending confrontation was soon resolved as the frightened officials had to back down and release those under arrest. Soon it was decided to transfer the storehouse to another place. But before that was done, believers began to follow each other to the mosque, and soon prayers were heard in the half-delapidated building.

There were numerous incidents of this kind. The authorities realised that the return of mosques to the believers was inevitable, as

Figure 17. Hakim al-Termezi ensemble (XI–XV c.) old Termez

was the growing process of religious enlightenment, which could only be stopped by reprisals and persecution.

The local communist bosses (most of whom remained Moslem in their day-to-day lives), on seeing that they would not receive Moscow's backing in these matters, for bigwigs in the capital were quite liberal towards religious renaissance, preferred to look through their fingers at the activities of the enlighteners. Moreover, from having opposed enlightenment, the communist authorities switched to supporting it, and even attempted to stand at the head of it.

In a way, it could be said that two processes merged – enlightenment from below and reorientation of the communist leadership from fighting Islam to restoring Moslem culture, supporting religious and national traditions, and developing religious education.

New attitude to religion

The new attitude to religion became evident in speeches by the first secretaries of the Central Asian communist parties, in their participation in religious festivals, and in the abolition of harsh atheistic propaganda. We refer to the *Programme of Action of the Communist Party of Uzbekistan* (draft) published at the end of 1990, which said, in part: 'While adhering to scientific materialistic world outlook, the Communist Party dissociates itself from the voluntaristic actions of the past against religion . . . The Party is ready to cooperate with religious organisations in asserting human values and welcomes their participation in socio-political and cultural life.'[3] Since 1990 and 1991, observance of religious festivals (declared to be holidays) has been allowed in all Central Asian republics. Special rooms for prayers are allotted at industrial enterprises and offices.

(One of the authors of this book was witness to an episode in Turkmenistan in 1972. On the Birthday of Prophet Muhammad, the Egyptian officers studying at a special military training centre there broadcast through a loudspeaker a prayer for the occasion. *Suras* from the Koran read over the radio for all town residents to hear shocked the local authorities. The man in charge of the radio studio who let the Egyptians in was severely punished.) Since 1990 a loudly pronounced word of God has no longer frightened the communist administration.

Central Asian newspapers, among which were numerous new 'independent' ones, although controlled by the authorities, wrote at length about the reconstruction of old mosques and the building of new ones, and about the opening of *madrasas* and entire Islamic institutes. The Tajik Islamic Institute, named after Imom-al-Termizi, and in which about 150 students are studying was built very quickly. Incidentally, the construction work was supervised by a spiritual leader – Imam-Khatib Usmon Rakhimdzhonov.[4]

In Tashkent, the famous Tokhta Boi Mosque was fully restored after it was given over to the Ecclesiastical Board. This big mosque stands in the centre of the city, not far from its biggest market. At Friday prayers, the number of parishioners is so great that the police have to divert the traffic.[5]

We have cited only two examples. Concerning figures for each of the Central Asian republics, not to mention the region as a whole, the total number of mosques is impossible to count. According to some figures, in Uzbekistan alone about 3,000 mosques had been restored or built anew by the beginning of 1992. In Tajikistan 130 big (that is, main) town mosques were operating in 1992.[6] There are up to 500 mosques functioning in comparatively sparsely populated

Turkmenistan. Two hundred mosques and two *madrasas* are working in Kyrgyzstan. There are more mosques operating now in Kazakhstan, too. It is indeed difficult to give an exact figure for the number of mosques, for today, just as in the distant past, there is a mosque in each neighbourhood, without counting district and town mosques. In many of them, a small school is attached to the mosque and attended by children born during the 1980s.

New *madrasas* are opening everywhere, and recently Islamic institutes and centres have begun to function: the already mentioned Imom-al-Termizi Islamic Institute in Tajikistan and the Tashkent Islamic Institute named after Imam al-Bukhari. The latter has special women's courses with up to 400 girl students. Religious education in Central Asia has ceased to be a privilege of men. Women's Islamic courses have opened at several *madrasas*. In Uzbekistan, there are such courses attached to the Begmur-Kazakh Madrasa in Kashkadarya District, attended by about 100 girls. Studies there are so popular that the *madrasa* heads opened several branches for these courses in neighbouring small towns and villages.

Since late 1989, bookshops in Central Asia have received more books on religion written in Arabic, Persian and local languages. A great number of them are written in Arabic and Persian scripts. In the past, such books, crumpled and torn, could be seen only in bazaars and in small shops, or were lying on the very ground, mixed up with old junk, whereas now everyone can buy a good book on religion published in Beirut, Cairo or Tehran. True, there are many buyers who can hardly read what is written in the book, for their knowledge of Arabic is poor. But how gratifying it is to have in one's house *Stories about Prophet Muhammad's Life* or, say, a book on *The Greatness and Future of Islamic Civilisation.*

As well as books, Moslem instructors come to Central Asia from Iran, Pakistan, Iraq, Saudi Arabia and Kuwait. Among them are professional preachers, theologians and those who simply take it upon themselves to assume the role of missionaries, explaining to Tajiks, Uzbeks, Turkmens and other Central Asian peoples the subtleties of Islamic philosophy, interpreting the Koran, and telling them about Moslem life abroad. Sometimes, the dissemination of religious knowledge is conducted by Arab postgraduates and even students studying in the former USSR. (All this reminds one, to a certain extent, of the situation in Algeria in the first half of the 1960s, when the country was 'suddenly' flooded by teachers and instructors from Egypt, who were teaching the Algerians everything – from Arabic to the principles of building a socialist society and the Shariah foundations.)

Gifts from Moslem countries

Since the late 1980s, active aid at government level has been rendered to their brethren in faith by Saudi Arabia, Kuwait, the United Arab Emirates, Pakistan, Iran, Turkey and Jordan.

At first, they sent religious literature. King Fahd of Saudi Arabia sent one million copies of the Koran to the Moslems of Central Asia as a gift. In addition, he also gave 400,000 disposable syringes, which are no less important for the inhabitants of Central Asia than books on religion. Large sums began pouring in from abroad for the construction of new mosques. A question was raised recently about replanning Central Asian cities in accordance with Islamic architectural standards. This was a subject of talks with Abd al-Baki Ibrahim, President of the Cairo Centre of Architectural and Construction Research, who promised to supply Uzbekistan with appropriate designs under a project to be financed by Saudi Arabia.[7]

Yet, in 1990 and 1991, the authorities, evidently from force of inertia, began talking about the need for atheistic propaganda and even adopted corresponding decisions. In June 1991, the Ideological Commission of the Central Committee of the Communist Party of Uzbekistan held a meeting at which the leaders of a number of regions – Andizhan, Bukhara, Kashkadarya (precisely where women's courses were opened at a *madrasa*), Namangan, and Samarkand – were criticised for weakening atheistic propaganda.The danger of growing religiousness among young people and the proliferation of a system of religious education was specially emphasised. 'School pupils are taught religion at home by self-styled teachers who have no right to do this. And students sympathise with believers,' K. Y. Yusupov, Secretary of the Central Committee of the Communist Party, said with indignation.[8] Anti-religious decrees were adopted at the time in Tajikistan and other republics, too.

'The activity of the clergy and its politicisation are growing; they have now an outlet to broad audiences through the mass media,' the First Secretary of the Tajik Communist Party, Kahar Mahkamov, said at the 21st Congress of the Party – its last. 'There is a trend toward an increase in the number of religious institutions, and the broadening of publishing and missionary activity, especially Moslem . . . At the same time,' he went on, 'atheistic work has been neglected.'[9] Incidentally, Kahar Mahkamov was the only one of the Central Asian leaders to admit publicly that he was an atheist, for which he was immediately punished by the Head of the Tajik Moslems, Akbar Turanjzoda, who declared that Mahkamov would be denied Moslem burial after his death.

Mention should. be made of an odd event. It was precisely in

Central Asia during the upsurge of Islamic renaissance that probably
the last monument to Lenin was erected. This was in April 1991, in
the Uzbek town of Yangibazar, on the eve of the birth anniversary of
the leader of Bolshevik revolution.

Having joined the religious educational activity the Communist
authorities did everything possible to control this process. Two trends
have become evident. On the one hand, the authorities support such
activity by the clergy. On the other, they obstruct the work of
independent enlighteners, thus continuing the policy aimed at
controlling Islam.

Enlightenment is also organically intertwined with nationalistic
views, just as the idea of national revival is intertwined with Islam. This
phenomenon has been noted by many scholars of Islam and
Kremlinologists. A scholar from Israel, Yaacov Ro'i, writes that 'The
Central Asians, and particularly the intellectual élites among them . . .
are rediscovering the region's traditional culture. This attaches them
further to Islam, which is the leitmotiv in traditional Central Asian
literature and philosophy.'[10]

The ideas of enlightenment feature in the programmes not only of
the Islamic political parties which came into being in 1990–1, but also
of such organisations as the Uzbek 'Birlik', Tajik 'Rastokhez', Kazakh
'Azat', and others.

In connection with enlightenment, the stepping up of social and
political activity under the slogans of Islam, and also an interest in the
political and economic concepts widespread in Moslem society
abroad, a question arises as to whether it would be possible to speak
about the revival of reformist tendencies on the Moslem territory of
the former USSR. The point is to restore the trend of Islamic thought,
which has been interrupted for more than a quarter of a century, and
also to reinterpret the classical heritage of the reformers –
Muhammad Abduh and Jamal ad-Din al-Afghani. This process has
already begun, as is shown, among other things, by numerous
publications and speeches by theologians, scholars and public figures.

Its should be noted that neither Abduh nor al-Afghani were the
most popular authors in Central Asia during that period. Incidentally,
their books could often be seen in personal libraries and in
bookshops. But an interest in works by Islamic fundamentalists –
Hassan al-Banna, Sayyed Qutb, Yusuf al-Kardavi, and, of course,
Khomeini – has sharply increased. Their works have been quickly
translated into Uzbek and Tajik. In Turkic Central Asia, a translation
of a book into one local language will contribute substantially to its
access to other regions. As for the Tajiks, they understand the
language of Khomeini without any translation.

However, while the trend of enlightenment was becoming more

and more pronounced, and the Moslems of Central Asia were getting used to the fact that their Islam was no longer an 'instrument of class oppression', and while Moslem festivals were turning from 'illegal' into national, and the secular Soviet authorities were reorientating themselves from persecution of religion to its glorification, a new trend was growing rapidly in Central Asian Islam, namely, its politicisation, the emergence of Moslem religion as an independent political force.

Notes

1. Cited in *al-Azhar* (in Arabic), April 1990, p. 957.
2. *Islamskiye Novosti*, Makhachkala, 19 November 1990.
3. *Pravda Vostoka*, Tashkent, 20 November 1990.
4. *Narodnaya Gazeta*, Dushanbe, 5 April 1991.
5. *Pravda Vostoka*, 5 April 1991.
6. *Narodnaya Gazeta*, 11 June 1992.
7. *Narodnaya Slovo*, Tashkent, 28 April 1992.
8. *Pravda Vostoka*, 7 July 1991.
9. *Kommunist Tajikistana*, 25 May 1990.
10. Yaacov Ro'i, *The Islamic Influence on Nationalism in Soviet Central Asia. Problems of Communism*, July–August, 1990, p. 59.

CHAPTER FIVE

ISLAM AND POLITICS

The world began to talk about 'Islamic renaissance' in the USSR, first and foremost, in connection with the emergence, or rather return, of Islam on to the political stage, but not in connection with the strengthening of enlightenment tendencies.

There is nothing extraordinary in the participation of Islam in politics. Islam is the most politicised religion in the world. Its political engagement has long become quite customary. Let us recall the successes of Islamists in such a secular country as Algeria, where the Islamic Salvation Front, having scored a brilliant election victory, would inevitably have come to power constitutionally, had it not been for the intervention of the Algerian army. The Islamists emerged victorious at parliamentary elections in Kuwait in 1992. There are several Islamist ministers in the government of Jordan. Islamists are in power in Iran and Afghanistan. The presidents and governments of almost all Moslem countries have to reckon with the Islamic opposition. And it is hardly likely that Islam will renounce its political presence in the near future. On the contrary, this will probably increase. Central Asia is becoming, or rather has already become, a hub of Islamism.

During the first years of *perestroika* in the Soviet Union (1985–9), Islam's participation in politics seemed quite unexpected to many people. In any case, it was not easy, at first glance to find a place in the political make-up of Soviet society which could be taken by the Islamists. General passiveness, the absolute domination of the Communist Party, the complete lack of political freedom, rendered it impossible for the adherents of political Islam to carry on serious political activity.

Besides, the official Moslem clergy have opposed, and continue to oppose, participation in politics, considering it impermissible to use religion for political purposes. But let us make a reservation: assimilating the concept of 'clergy' into Islam is rather relative. There is not an official clerical hierarchy similar to that existing in Christianity. Islam does not recognise mediators between the Almighty and the believer, either. Any Moslem who, from the point of view of his community, knows the Koran better than others, is familiar with the Shariah and whose behaviour is fully in line with the strict standards of Islamic morality, can organise the religious life of Moslems, conduct the prayer and read sermons. In actual fact, the *imams, muezzins, qadis* and *muftis* represent a special caste of the clergy, which can well be compared with the clergy of other religions. This is all the more so since there have been, since ages past, special educational establishments in Moslem countries for training 'professional' priests.

The political indifference of the clergy in Central Asia is conditioned not only by the fear of losing their authority, but also by the fact that their present generation was educated in the spirit of secularisation. True, 'departure from politics' has never prevented the higher echelon of the clergy from cooperating quite actively with the authorities, nor from taking part in various quasi-political campaigns and the international activity of the Soviet government. Nor has it prevented them from being elected to various representative bodies, including the Congress of USSR People's Deputies. All this explains why it was not the clergy who became the leading force of Islamic renaissance, let alone of Islam's engagement in politics.

Leading role of fundamentalists

The leading role was played by the fundamentalists, who existed in a comparatively small number on the political map of the Soviet Union as far back as the 1970s. They proved able to traverse very rapidly the path from clandestine gatherings to mass meetings, the creation of parties, and even participation in the formation of administrative structures. In Tajikistan, fundamentalists entered the government for several months in 1992.

The activity of the religious forces after 1985, like the emergence of the opposition in general, was caused by an overall worsening of the economic situation. On the other hand, fundamentalism was a natural, if inevitable, form of Islamic renaissance in a country (now countries) where, for three-quarters of a century, Islam was regarded by the authorities as a force hostile to man. Fundamentalism has, to a degree, become the *alter ego* of Islamic enlightenment.

Another reason for the stepping up of Islam's political activity was national revival. The authors share the view expressed by John Esposito, an American scholar, that nationalism and Islam are closely intertwined in each state of Central Asia and mutually stimulate each other. National rebirth is indissolubly linked with religious renaissance, and it is difficult to say which element is the dominating one.

Without attempting to analyse thoroughly fundamentalism as a socio-political and ideological-cultural phenomenon or to argue with some of their colleagues – political scientists and scholars of Islam – the authors, nevertheless, deem it necessary to outline briefly their concept of fundamentalism.

Fundamentalism is basically an attempt to evolve a model of social structure relying, to the greatest extent possible, on the values of one of the great regional civilisations – Christian, Moslem, or Buddhist (the paradigm of civilisation may differ). In this civilisational heritage, religion is playing the key role, which, in the fundamentalists' view, primarily regulates relations between people, with due consideration of course, to their concrete national features. And not only does it regulate personal relations, but also those in the spheres of the economy, politics and government of the state. This is a model of social structure in which, as its ideologists believe, the potential of civilisation is realised best and which corresponds to the moral standards, political culture, spiritual ideas and psychology of each individual in a given civilisation.

Fundamentalism is not an exclusively Moslem phenomenon. It emerges as an ideological and political current in any regional civilisation, which was aptly demonstrated by the French scholar Gilles Kepel in his book *La Revanche de Dieu*. He wrote: 'Such religious movements are still flourishing in the world . . . Today the world has ended the era of industrialisation and entered into a new epoch, in which social relations . . . are undergoing transformations which we do not know as yet how to define. The emergence of new religious movements may help us in this.'[1]

We would like to point out why Islamic fundamentalism particularly, is especially noticeable against the general background, so much so that the very word 'fundamentalism' has for the last decade and a half been associated with Islam. This can be explained by the fact that Islamic fundamentalism is extremely active and politicised. This, in turn, is due to the failure of alien models of social development – European and socialist – in the Moslem world. As a result, the position of the people who maintain that the only way out is to return to the roots of Islamic civilisation, has strengthened in the Moslem world. It is not for nothing that the phenomenon known as fundamentalism is termed '*usuliya*' in Arabic, from the word '*asl*' which means 'root'. The 'explosion' of fundamentalism in the Moslem world was a kind of answer to the intrusion into traditional society of other political principles, values and behavioural standards formed in an alien sphere.

Incidentally, there are grounds for speaking about the growth of fundamentalist trends in Russia too, where Russian Orthodox fundamentalism becomes a reaction to the failures of the economic reform, the contradictory process of democratisation and the general deterioration of the living standards of the population. So today, as far as the Commonwealth of Independent States (CIS) is concerned, one could speak not only of Islamic fundamentalism, but of fundamentalism *per se.*

During the first three years of *perestroika*, Islamic fundamentalist tendencies were not clearly enunciated. Fundamentalism was not a consolidated movement and had no organisational structures at the time. One could speak of isolated manifestations of fundamentalism in the developing political struggle. The fundamentalists had no political leaders to reckon with, and did not put forward any radical demands expressing any clear-cut political programme.

On the other hand, fundamentalism reflected the desire of certain social groups for self-expression and also for the well-articulated striving for self-realisation. Besides this, some fundamentalist groups were financed by mafia structures using Islam for their own, purely selfish interests.

Party of Islamic Rebirth

Paradoxically, the first attempt to create a general Moslem political movement with a fundamentalist trend took place in Russia, where the party of Islamic Rebirth (PIR) 'suddenly' emerged, rather than in Central Asia, as one might have expected.

The constituent congress of the Party of Islamic Rebirth was held on 9 June 1990 in Astrakhan, a large administrative centre in the lower reaches of the greatest Russian river, the Volga. At first, the leadership of the party was dominated by representatives of the Tatar and Avar (the latter being a people inhabiting Daghestan) Moslem communities. One of the present leaders of the Tajik fundamentalists, Tajikistan's Vice-Premier Davlat Usmon, however, maintains that in Astrakhan more than half of the Congress delegates were Tajiks.

Ahmedkadi Akhtayev, a medical doctor and Avar by nationality, was elected Chairman of the party, and Valiahmed Sadur, a Moscow scientist, Tatar by nationality, became its press secretary and chief ideologist.

A number of premisses in the party's Programme give some idea of its ideology and strategic aims. 'The Party of Islamic Rebirth', the first paragraph of the Programme says, 'is a religious-political organisation uniting the Moslems who are actively propagating Islam, observe its rules and take part in religious-cultural, socio-political and economic life on the basis of the principles of Islam.' The party advocates, as it is said in paragraph 27 of the Programme, 'regulation of the excessive accumulation of wealth in the hands of the few on the basis of the Shariah'. In conclusion, the Programme emphasises that 'the invested schemes of social development have led mankind to a deep crisis in all spheres of life. We see salvation only in following the path of Allah.'[2] (This is a typically fundamentalist wording, characteristic of all Middle Eastern fundamentalists, from Egyptian Sayyed Qutb to the leader of the Libyan revolution Muammar Gaddafi.)

The party is a unique phenomenon in Soviet political life. It was actually the only religious party. Moreover, it openly proclaimed itself the party of all Moslems living on Soviet territory. Of course, three years later, one could speak about its failure to fulfil its strategic tasks. The party has not become a leading political force as an all-Union party, or later, within the CIS framework. However, it provided an impetus to the self-organisation of the Islamic political movement and stimulated the growth and dissemination of fundamentalism.

Naturally, the party leadership regarded Central Asia, where the revival of Islam was proceeding apace and which had experience, although rather limited, of Islam's participation in politics, as the most promising place for spreading its influence. Believing that it was possible to act legally, the party leadership intended to set up branches of the party in all Central Asian republics simultaneously.

However, the very first attempts met with sharp opposition from the authorities. The constituent conferences of the regional branches of the party in Tajikistan and Uzbekistan reads like a thriller.

From the start, it became clear that it would be impossible to hold a regional conference of the party in the Tajik capital, Dushanbe. The local authorities knew about the conferences and took all measures to disrupt it. All active supporters of the organisation of the Islamic Party in the republic were placed under surveillance. The question of the immediate banishment from Dushanbe of the party leaders who arrived for the conference was under consideration. Plans to shadow delegates at hotels were drawn up. The authorities prohibited club and cinema threatre managers from letting their premises for the conference. KGB officials kept mosques under constant surveillance, for fundamentalists and their guests could gather there. On the eve of the conference, state security agents detained several bearded young men as they left the mosques; the authorities thought a beard was a sure sign of adherence to the Islamic Party.

However, the Party, too, observed the rules of security. Quite unexpectedly for the authorities, the regional conference was transferred to one of the rural districts, an hour's drive from Dushanbe. The exact time and place were known only to a very limited circle of initiates. Tajik Islamists placed their men at city crossings to direct cars carrying the participants and guests of the conference.

In any case, the police were late: on 6 October 1990 the regional conference of the Party of Islamic Rebirth took place and formed its branch in Tajikistan.

The conference of the party held in Tashkent, the capital of Uzbekistan, in January 1991 faced even greater difficulties. The police and the KGB of Uzbekistan, bearing in mind the experience of their colleagues in Tajikistan, acted more resolutely. The conference was scheduled to begin on 26 January and on that day a plain-clothes policeman or KGB agent stood at the entrance to each mosque. Besides this, delegates to the conference were harassed at the railway station and airport. Although they did not arrest the delegates, the local authorities thought that the atmosphere of intimidation would have a depressing effect on party members and their supporters.

The conference began in a textile workers' club in the very centre of Tashkent. (The KGB discovered the exact location of the conference only after it began.)

While the police were gathering forces with a view to disrupting the conference, its participants managed to adopt the most important documents concerning the creation of a regional organisation and to elect its chairman. Then men of a special police unit broke into the club, dragged people from the hall and smashed the equipment of a cameraman trying to take pictures of the massacre. One of the police shouted insults at the Moslems and declared: 'Uzbekistan is the only place where Soviet power is preserved'.[3]

All the participants remanded in custody later appeared in 'court' where the role of judge was played by local officials sitting in the office of the head of the district department of the interior. They were all fined 300–500 roubles which was quite a big sum at the time. Information is available indicating that the entire operation for the prevention of the conference was controlled personally by Uzbekistan's President Islam Karimov.

But the task set by the party, namely to set up a regional organisation, was also accomplished in Tashkent.

It should be mentioned that, by that time, cells and branches of the party had appeared in many towns and republics of the northern Caucasus, Central Russia, in Moscow, Leningrad (now St Petersburg), in the Volga Region, the Urals and Siberia.

Cells, though very small, were formed in Turkmenistan, Kazakhstan

Figure 18. Shah-i Zinda Mausoleum (XIV c.), Samarkand

and even Kyrgyzstan as well as in Turkmenistan, Kazakhstan and even Kyrgyzstan, where the entire branch of the party consisted of four or five people, Uzbeks by nationality.

The relative success of the Party of Islamic Rebirth in Central Asia is due largely not only to the attractive character of its Programme, but also to the persecution and reprisals inflicted on it by the local authorities. This is one of the paradoxes of the Soviet domestic policy during *perestroika*: those who were persecuted most of all by the authorities enjoyed the greatest popularity among the people.

The Party of Islamic Rebirth was banned in three republics of Central Asia: Uzbekistan, Tajikistan and Turkmenistan. The Head of State, Islam Karimov of Uzbekistan and his colleague in Tajikistan, Kahar Mahkamov, came out against the party. The general opinion of the Soviet authorities was most aptly expressed by N. Ovezov, a high-ranking Turkmen official responsible for religious affairs at the Council of Ministers of Turkmenistan. He said: 'I can assure you, expressing the view of most Turkmens, that we don't need any parties of Moslem rebirth.'[4]

The institutionalised clergy have also come out against the Party of Islamic Rebirth. Mufti Muhammad Sodik Mohammed Yusef, Chairman of the Ecclesiastical Board of Moslems of Central Asia and Kazakhstan, said: 'There were attempts to form a Moslem party, something like a party of Moslem rebirth . . . The official clergy object to it. We consider that Islam by itself is a party which has existed for over 1,400 years already.'[5]

Another party which came into being at about the same time, and whose ideology had an imprint of fundamentalism, was the Islamic Party of Turkestan which claimed the right to speak on behalf of all Turkic peoples living on the territory of the USSR. Its appeal to fundamentalist ideals was but part of its ideological and political doctrine. This party did not have any decisive influence on the alignment of political forces. It remained practically unnoticed on the political scene of Central Asia. The Islamic Party of Turkestan was a kind of circle of intellectuals dreaming about the revival of Turkic ideas. This party disappeared just as inconspicuously as it emerged.

Both the secular authorities and the institutionalised clergy sensed, by their 'social instinct', the danger spelt for them in the rising religious political tide. Being afraid of fundamentalism, and at the same time fearing that open and frequent action against its adherents might have a negative effect on their prestige, the authorities resorted to the widespread practice of the communist regimes which was to ignore the problem. Apart from individual, sharply critical, remarks about the Party of Islamic Rebirth, the local press was practically silent on the question. At the time, it was mainly Russian, and mainly Moscow, journalists, who wrote about fundamentalism.

Nevertheless, some representatives of the Communist Party apparatus, and intellectuals collaborating with them, were increasingly coming to the conclusion that a more flexible approach to the Moslem opposition was needed. Indicative in this respect is an article which appeared in the magazine *Kommunist Uzbekistana* in 1990. Its author, I. Makatov, wrote that 'religious views and feelings have not only definite spiritual orientations, but also form the motives of man's social behaviour and programme him, as it were. This factor is being widely used by those adhering to fundamentalism with a view to enhancing the social purport of Islam.' Besides this, as the same author noted, there is a real danger in Moslem regions of religious extremist manifestations and confessional intolerance. A thought was expressed about a possible cooperation between the communists and the 'non-fundamentalist' part of the religious opposition, namely, the Moslem *tariqas*. All this required, in I. Makatov's view, 'the drawing of the *murids* into socio-cultural and educational undertakings and the establishment of a dialogue between them and the authorities'.[6]

A confrontation between the secular authorities and fundamentalists in Central Asia has become a permanent feature. Its was especially typical of Tajikistan, Uzbekistan, and, later, of Kazakhstan, and to a lesser degree, Kyrgyzstan and Turkmenistan. (In the latter, pro-fundamentalist sentiments are combined with full support for the legitimate President Saparmurad Niyazov.)

The struggle around the formation of regional organisations of the Party of Islamic Rebirth, and in fact around legalisation of the Islamic movement, ended in defeat for the Islamists. Nowhere in Central Asia was the party legalised. It has not become the basis for the general Moslem movement in Central Asia, even less so in the whole of the USSR. On the other hand, events connected with the party were milestones on the road to the emergence and consolidation of independent fundamentalist parties in individual republics, which subsequently became independent Moslem states.

Who supports the fundamentalists?

Who supports the fundamentalists and on which sections of the population does the fundamentalist movement rely? Judging by newspaper and magazine articles and information received by the authors directly from people sharing the ideas of the renaissance of Islam and its 'political presence', the slogans of fundamentalism are most popular among: (1) some students; (2) rural dwellers; (3) young men who have recently come to the towns from the countryside; (4) representatives of the traditionalist intelligentsia; (5) middle or lower sections of the clergy wishing to distance themselves from the higher echelon of Moslem priests.

A considerable part of the population indifferent to politics is psychologically predisposed to render a more-or-less significant support to fundamentalism. Fundamentalist phraseology attracts primarily those who are not connected with the modern sector of production. Workers and engineering and technical staff at industrial enterprises have not taken, and are not taking, any part in the fundamentalist movement. In contrast, there is a high percentage of rural dwellers and people from the spheres of service and trade among the adherents of fundamentalism.

Fundamentalism has the greatest influence on people in the 16 to 24-years-old age bracket. This may be connected with the striving for active self-assertion typical of people of that age. In older age groups, interest in fundamentalism diminishes. After 25 years of age, men are more preoccupied with their personal and family problems and are against the radical forms of political, including religious-political, self-assertion. It was not 30- and 40-year-old men who were most active at fundamentalist meetings but those over 60, past retirement, who again turn to politics. And they look with pleasure at their young grandchildren waving the green banner of the Prophet.

The reason for the popularity of fundamentalist slogans lies in disappointment with the policy pursued for decades by the communist authorities, which failed to result in a cardinal improvement in people's living standards. The war in Afghanistan dealt a heavy blow to the prestige of communist rule. Faith in the construction of socialist society suffered a no less serious defeat during the years of *perestroika*. The general economic decline, the disruption of the old familiar economic ties and the sharp reduction of social guarantees – all this caused great confusion among the Moslems, for the greater part of them failed to understand properly what the authorities wanted them to do. In any case, people began to understand that the Soviet version of the realisation of the socialist idea had been a fiasco. They instinctively felt that it was necessary to search for an alternative model. This hypothetical model was objectively and inevitably associated with Islam.

History repeats itself. In the late 1970s and early 1980s, the Moslem world became greatly disillusioned with almost all varieties of socialism – from Marxist to Arab. The failure of the Western version of progress led to the Islamic revolution in Iran. The degradation of the Arab types of socialism provoked millions of dissatisfied Moslems to take to the streets. They became convinced that neither European capitalism nor socialism brought in from Europe and adapted to the local conditions would save them. Consequently, salvation lay in Islam.

However, fundamentalism in the USSR, and later in the CIS, has its specific features conditioned by local factors which make it different from fundamentalism in the Middle East. In Arab states, Iran and other countries, the fundamentalists were opposed by the Westernised higher and middle sections of society. In Central Asia however, the Islamists were opposed by the communist structures, which for a long time used to advantage such concepts, so close to Islam, as 'social justice', 'collectivisim' and 'stable power'.

In a way, one could speak of a repetition – limited, of course – of the confrontation between communism and Islam during the 1920–30 period, when Marxist ideology, which had taken the form of a world revolution in the USSR (almost similar to the Islamic *jihad*), was trying to oust Islam from its own ideological and psychological niche: collectivism, social justice, authoritarianism. Today one could speak of a similar process, but inverted: the adherents of Islam are trying to prove that the communists exploited Islamic standards and values, but in fact made efforts to destroy Islamic civilisation and culture. And again both sides are frequently waging their campaigns under similar slogans. In addition, the communists are intimidating the local democrats, saying that if they, the communists, depart, Moslem fanatics will come to take their place.

After abortive attempts to create a uniform Moslem political movement, the fundamentalists 'left for their national quarters', and a fundamentalist centre (or centres) came into being in almost all republics.

Fundamentalists' strength in Tajikistan

The fundamentalist movement has become strongest and most influential in Tajikistan. It is represented there by the Party of Islamic Rebirth and also by some local fundamentalist groups (often called Wahhabite).

The Party of Islamic Rebirth of Tajikistan has emerged from a regional organisation. It was officially registered as a Tajik party in November 1991. (It should be noted that this was the first and only instance of the legalisation of a religious party in Central Asia.) The ceremony of the handing of the registration certificate to the party's President, Muhammadsharif Khimmatzoda, was photographed for the official newspaper *Narodnaya Gazeta*.

The official permission for the functioning of the party has put an end to the many months of struggle between the authorities and the Islamic Party, whose side was taken by the head of the Tajik clergy Akbar Turanjzoda. This example of cooperation between the fundamentalists and the official clergy is unique in the history of Central Asia. This circumstance contributed to the consolidation of the Islamic forces and at the same time restrained the opponents of the Party of Islamic Rebirth.

Having emerged from 'underground', the party has become the leading force of the political opposition, uniting the national democratic movement, Rastokhez, the Democratic Party of Tajikistan, Lalyi Badakhshon, and a number of smaller political groupings.

In the presidential elections of December 1991, the coalition of these parties put forward one candidate, Davlat Khudonazarov, a well-known film director, popular for his democratic views, and a staunch opponent of the communists. In this way, Tajikistan witnessed the unique experience of close cooperation between forces which are far apart in values and political convictions: the democrats and the Islamists. Davlat Khudonazarov's candidature for election was not prevented by the fact that he belonged to the Pamir Shiite sect of Ismailis of whom Moslems living in the valleys and plains have always been suspicious.

However, the opposition candidate lost the elections. Power remained in the hands of President Rakhmon Nabiyev, a communist, who obtained 57 per cent of the votes, as against 31 per cent cast for Khudonazarov. The opposition declared that the election results had been rigged and called on the people for further struggle against Nabiyev. Various sections of the population were drawn into the struggle between the president and the opposition. They called meetings on two squares in Dushanbe: Ozodi (supporters of the opposition) and Shahidon (supporters of the president). The age-old differences and rivalry between the north (President Nabiyev's country) and the south have become sharply aggravated.

As is known, it is representatives of the Khodzhent clan who have always held dominant positions in Tajikistan. (In the years of Soviet rule Khodzhent was renamed Leninabad; today the towns' former name has been restored.) Tajikistan's southern regions have always considered themselves passed over by the people of Khodzhent. This was one of the reasons why the PIR's support was particularly strong in the south. The confrontation which lasted throughout the winter and early spring of 1992 demonstrated the strength of the opposition, above all that of the Islamists, who, in the opinion of numerous experts, have become the most influential force in society.

PIR activists were principal speakers at rallies decorated with green banners and slogans. Incidentally, the fundamentalists together with the clergy held in check extremists from groups not controlled by the PIR.

The PIR leaders assert that it was through their efforts that the authorities' intention to provoke the rallying people was thwarted. This statement appears to have a ring of truth about it, for the power structures subordinated to Rakhmon Nabiyev were obviously interested in creating disturbances which might be used as a convenient pretext for dispersing the opposition rallies.

By April 1992, it became evident that neither side in the conflict had the necessary clout to win a victory. Rakhmon Nabiyev agreed a compromise: a coalition government in which the opposition received one-third of the ministerial posts, including those of the defence and security portfolios, was set up. Davlat Usmon, deputy chairman of the PIR, was appointed vice-premier.

Despite the limited character of the PIR's success, it should be noted that the event that took place in Tajikistan was a landmark in the history of the young Central Asian states. For the first time ever, an Islamist party was allowed the reins of government.

Fundamentalist influence in Uzbekistan

This was of great significance for the neighbouring republics, especially for Uzbekistan, whose president, Islam Karimov, quite reasonably regarded the elevation of the Tajik fundamentalists as a serious threat to the stability of his state and to his own welfare.

Certainly, the potential of the fundamentalist movement in Uzbekistan is less than that in neighbouring Tajikistan; yet its influence has been growing there as well. In Uzbekistan, however, there are no forces that can constitute the nucleus of this movement. The influence of the local Islamic Rebirth Party is rather limited. Nor does it have sufficiently authoritative leaders, of the calibre of Muhammadsharif Khimmatzoda. The official clergy, fully supporting the president, comes out resolutely against the Islamists. Finally, no coalition of opposition forces has been formed in Uzbekistan. There are numerous contradictions between two leading opposition parties, the Erk and the Birlik, and the Islamists.

Naturally, the Uzbek Democrats recognise the great significance of Islam for the cause of national rebirth. Passages to this effect are to be found both in the policy documents of the two parties and in statements made by their leaders. For example, Muhammad Salih, chairman of the Erk, who as Islam Karimov's rival in the race for the presidency, said that, in the event of his success, he 'would not form an Islamic republic', but that he was 'ready to do everything in order to open every road to religious education'.[7] Neither the Erk nor the Birlik, however, intend to pull 'chestnuts out of the fire' for the fundamentalists, and both of them believe that their own resources will be quite sufficient to oppose the People's Democratic Party, which is now in power in Uzbekistan. At the same time, neither the Birlik

Figure 19. Sufi Mazar of Hakim al-Termezi (IX c.), Termez

nor the Erk wish to tie their hands by active cooperation with the fundamentalists. Even less do they share their views about the 'Islamic future' of Uzbekistan.

The Democrats are keeping their distance from the fundament-alists, particularly since it is not the Islamic Rebirth Party of Uzbekistan, but the Adolat (Justice) organisation, which came into being in October 1991, that is becoming the most influential force among the Islamic activisits.

The emergence of the Adolat is a direct result of the sharp deterioration of the population's living standards, sky-rocketing prices at town bazaars, and the wave of crime and hooliganism in the streets of Uzbek towns which the local militia has proved unable to check.

The nucleus of the Adolat is composed of special *makhalla* ('*makhalla*' being a town neighbourhood in Uzbekistan) volunteer squads for maintaining public order within 'their own' neighbour-hoods. These same squads, consisting of strong young men, have brought the markets' pricing system under their control, preventing market traders from jacking prices up to sky-high levels inaccessible to average urban dwellers. Gradually, the leaders of the squads reached the conclusion that they should coordinate their actions. The results

were not long in coming. Somehow or other, in the towns where the
Adolat is active, there has been a sharp decline in crime and a drop in
prices at markets.

The Adolat's area of activity includes Namanga, where the
organisation was initially set up, Fergana, and also a number of towns
and populated localities in the Fergana Valley. In the spring of 1992,
the Adolat made an abortive attempt to extend its area of activity to
Tashkent.

The Adolat has firmly established itself in those districts where the
level of the population's religiosity is particularly high and where
groups of Islamic activists operated illegally as long ago as before the
beginning of *perestroika*. Besides, it is easy to see that the Fergana
Valley is the place where tension is highest and where economic and
social conflicts which threaten to shatter relatively prosperous
Uzbekistan from the inside are accumulating.

Having set itself up as guarantor of social justice, the Adolat
desperately needed the sanction of men of authority in religion, who
saw in this organisation a potentially powerful instrument for
upholding Islamic morality and Islamic traditions. Besides this, among
the activitists and members of the Adolat there are many young
people who are interested in Islam and who view the formation of an
Islamic state as, perhaps, the only possible way out of the generally
grave situation. It is no accident that numerous members of this
organisation, including some of its leaders, openly admit that their
organisation is a local variant of the Moslem brotherhood. In
describing the activists of the Adolat, some journalists – sometimes not
without reason – call them 'guardians of Islam' or an 'Islamic security
service'.[8]

In several towns, there have appeared volunteers seeing to it that
women do not wear 'immodest clothes' and that men observe more
strictly various rules set by Islam.

But, having voluntarily taken on the duties of a vice squad for
enforcing Islamic morals, the Adolat's activists began to claim the role
of a political organisation. In December 1991, they entered into
conflict with the administration when they took part in mass actions of
the people of Namangan, who demanded of Islam Karimov that a
public centre for studying the Koran be set up in the building of the
former Namangan Regional Committee of the Communist (now
People's Democratic) Party of Uzbekistan.

Within a few months, the Adolat grew into a substantial force
capable of influencing the general situation in Uzbekistan. Its
influence proved so strong that already in February 1992 the Adolat,
together with the Birlik, the Erk and the Islamic Rebirth Party, was
included in the list of organisations which were to take part in

negotiations with the president of Uzbekistan. The negotiations were planned to take place in Namangan. There are several versions of what happened next. According to one of them, the meeting was disrupted by representatives of Namangan, including supporters of the Adolat, who were outraged by a reshuffle of the region's leadership carried out by the president without regard for the opinion of the local public and religious authorities. According to another, Islam Karimov, outraged by the bluntness of the opposition's demands, refused to hold any talks with it himself. (There is yet another story, namely, that supporters of the Adolat brought pressure to bear upon the president so resolutely that he was compelled to flee from Namangan. This account, however, seems more likely to belong in legend.)

What is known for certain is that, following the abortive attempt to hold negotiations, Islam Karimov shifted from dialogue with the opposition to tough opposition to it. A few days after his return from Namangan, he ordered the arrest of the leaders of the Adolat and several of its activists, having accused the Adolat and with it the Islamic Rebirth Party, of extremism. True, there is another explanation for the real motive behind these harsh measures: by that time substantial oil deposits had been discovered not far from Namangan, and the Uzbek leadership intended to enlist the aid of foreign – in the first place, US – companies in exploiting them. Accordingly, it aimed to show that it was in full control of the situation and could ensure political stability in the republic and that it would on no account permit any manifestations by Islamic fundamentalists, who are much disliked in the West.

Somehow or other, the first clash between the opposition, including the Islamists, and the Uzbek administration ended clearly in the latter's favour. It is also quite clear that this clash was by no means the last, and that Islamic fundamentalism, alongside the secular opposition, has become part and parcel of political life in Uzbekistan.

Fundamentalists in Kazakhstan

Kazakhstan also has its fundamentalists, although they are less conspicuous. They are represented by the Alash National Freedom Party. Unlike 'classical fundamentalism', the Alashites are advocates of a synthesis of the ideas of Islamism and Turkism. This alone is sufficient to make the Alash a unique kind of political grouping, different from all other parties – both those in office and those in opposition – in the Moslem region of the CIS.

It should be noted that the idea of Turkism has taken deep enough roots in the political life of that region (naturally, with the exception of Tajikistan). In the most varied strata of society, there is a growing conviction of the need to strengthen, within the general Turkic ethnic and cultural area, all-round cooperation of the Turkic peoples, who, acting jointly, may become an immense geopolitical force. On the other hand, at a governmental level, the idea of Turkism is concretised, in particular, in a desire to borrow (since copying is hardly possible) certain fragments of the model of development proposed by Turkey, the indisputable leader of the Turkic world.

In both these cases, however, Turkism appears mostly in a secular form. And, although the advocates of the drawing together of the Turkic peoples name Islam among the features common to all of them, none of them elevates it to an absolute nor links the idea of Turkism with Islamic fundamentalism. None, that is, except the small, yet highly energetic, Alash Party. Aron Atabek, chairman of the party, interprets its name as 'Red Wolf' (symbol of the Turkic peoples) or as 'Victor'.[9]

The Alash came into being in 1990. At the time, it was composed of a few dozen young men, mostly students. According to Aron Atabek, the average age of the Alashites is 22 to 24 years. The party has its cells in the south of the republic. Today, its total membership is about 3,000.

Having initially declared themselves the successors of the 'old' Alash Party, which was active before the October Revolution of 1917 and which retired from the political scene in 1918 (the Alash being merged into the Russian Communist Party – Bolsheviks), the Alashites proceeded to lay greater emphasis on Islam, stressing in every way the unity of Islamic and Turkic rebirth. They are firmly convinced that Islam is inseparably linked with politics. The Alashites come out against ethnic nationalism, for they believe that the nationalism of individual ethnic groups objectively opposes the idea of Turkic solidarity.

The Alash Party regards the Kazakhs, above all, specifically as a 'fragment' of the Turkic people. In this respect, the Alashites' stand can be compared with the views of the Azerbaijan Turkists associated with Abulfez Elchibey, today's President of Azerbaijan. (Elchibey's Turkism is even more radical: he is known to regard his own people, the Azerbaijanis, as part of the Turks.)

The Alash's main aims, alongside with the 'achievement by Kazakhstan of the real status of an independent ethnic state', are 'integration and propagation of the ideas of Turkic unity and Moslem solidarity', and also 'national rebirth of Kazakhstan as the historical nucleus of the future unified Islamic Turkic state, Great Turkestan'.[10]

The Alash's ideology can be described by the following triad: Islam – Turkism – democracy. The notable feature of this triad is that it is Islam that stands in the first place (which makes it possible to speak about the Alash as an Islamist organisation). Democracy stands third, which is also quite significant. As is known, one of the principles of the fundamentalist ideology is categorical non-acceptance of the idea of democracy, which they regard as a purely Western concept quite alien to Islam. Such a trend has been observed among some of the Alashites as well. In the end, however, it was another, more flexible, point of view whose proponents believe it not only possible, but even necessary, to combine fundamentalism with democractic principles, that prevailed. True, they sometimes find it difficult to explain what is the best way to achieve this.

Thus it is Turkism bordered with Islam on one side and democracy on the other which constitutes the ideological basis of the 'new Alashites'. They come out against the communist system, which, in their view, still continues to exist in Kazakhstan, and are for the development of their state on the basis of a market economy. The Alash Party believes that 'Turkism is an absolute genetic factor that unites all the Turkic peoples; it constitutes the basis of the language, thinking, ethnopsychology and ethnoculture of the Turks.'[11]

The Alash makes up for its small membership by bustling activity, staging both large and small rallies in various towns of Kazakhstan. The Alash regards as its achievement the fact that its meetings – at any rate, so its leader says – are attended by non-Kazakhs as well, that is, by Russians, Ukrainians and Germans who support the Red Wolves' demand for democratisation of social and political life, the removal of former communists from power, and so on.

A major focus of the Alash's activity is the struggle against the collaborationist section of the Moslem clergy headed by Ratbek Naysanbayev, Mufti of Kazakhstan. He, the head of the Moslem Religious Board of Kazakhstan, is an ardent supporter of President Nursultan Nazarbayev. In addition, he has more than once spoken against any mixing of Islam with politics whatsoever and has criticised the Alash.

In December 1991, the Majlis (National Congress) of the Moslems of Kazakhstan took the decision to remove the *mufti* from office. Numerous accusations were brought against him: he was charged with corruption, with spending the funds of the Moslem community on himself, with wrecking the system of religious education, etc. During the altercation at the mosque when Ratbek Nysanbayev denied the charges brought against him and was afterwards compelled to leave the building, a scandal erupted, followed by a minor skirmish. According to official reports, the fist fight, during which the *mufti* had his arm broken, was started by the Alashites, for which they were subsequently punished. The members of the Alash, however, maintain that nothing of the kind in fact occurred and that the clash was provoked by supporters of the *mufti* and militiamen in plain clothes.

The brush at the mosque served as a pretext for the arrest of a number of Alash members, including several girls, and marked the beginning of active persecution of the party. The republic's leadership declared the Alash unconstitutional. Proceedings were initiated against some of its members. As a result of these developments, Aron Atabek, chairman of the party, was compelled to move to Moscow, from where he submitted a request for political asylum to the president of Azerbaijan. (It should be noted that this was the first case of this type in the CIS.) Naturally, the party's activity slackened after the departure of its leader.

At the same time, it should be said that the scale of harassment to which the party is being subjected hardly accords with the level of influence it has in Kazakhstan today. At present, the Alash does not constitute a serious danger for President Nazarbayev. Kazakhstan's ruling circles, however, are aware that, as economic difficulties are aggravated and as inter-ethnic relations deteriorate, the ideas being disseminated by the Alash grow ever more attractive. The synthesis of Turkism and Islamism may become the basis for a broad-scale movement capable of growing into a leading political force.

The ruling establishment of Central Asia and Kazakhstan has always been aware of the potential danger posed to it by the fundamentalist movement. One can even speak not so much about former communist bureaucrats' rational comprehension of Islam as about their instinctive fear of fundamentalism in which, by faultless intuition, they sensed their chief rival long before political Islam became organised in the form of parties and groupings.

Their intuition did not fail them, as is eloquently attested by the developments in Tajikistan where the Party of Islamic Rebirth participated in the government coalition in the period between the spring and autumn of 1992. During that period the fundamentalists strengthened their positions in Uzbekistan as well. Not only is the social basis for the spread of fundamentalism not becoming any narrower, but it will quite probably be expanding.

Besides parties and movements in Central Asia, there are also voluntary cultural societies whose views are quite close, or similar to, those of the fundamentalists. By way of example, we will cite the Sunnah Society in Turkmenistan. It is conducting an active campaign for the restoration of strict Islamic morality; in particular, it demands the restriction or banning of the broadcasting of some of the Central Television programmes which, as Ishankuli Madzhidov, the leader of the Sunnah, believes, make 'people fall ill both mentally and physically'.[12] There are also several other, smaller associations with a similar ideological orientation. A similar picture emerges in Kyrgyzstan where there is no Islamic political movement, but where there are also religious societies whose members condemn the penetration into the republic of ideas that are alien to Islam. The most radical stand, in this respect, is taken by the Islamic Centre of Kyrgyzstan whose head, Saiddzhan-Kamalov, clearly gravitates toward fundamentalism.

But then, as is known, the former party *nomenklatura*, whose just like the Islamic conservatives, speak about democracy as being alien to the traditions of Moslem society, are also against adopting anything 'foreign'.

Representatives of the pro-communist wing of the Russian nationalists 'of the native soil' (Russian version of fundamentalism), who renounce democracy (which they, like their Moslem counterparts, believe to be alien to the Russian Orthodox people), agree in a way with Islamic fundamentalist sentiments. Today, the so-called Russian patriotic newspapers willingly publish materials prepared by champions of the Islamic way of life.

Messianism and anti-foreignism

It is no accident that Moslem fundamentalism, Russian nationalism 'of the native soil' and communism have come to terms with each other. And this is not just a result of the political situation, even though this is the most conspicuous feature on the surface of public life in the former USSR. There are more profound reasons. The fact is that the communist and fundamentalist (Islamic and Russian Orthodox) ideas have two points in common: messianism and 'anti-foreignism'. The postulation of an 'us–them' dichotomy, the 'them' inevitably meaning Europeans with a different value orientation, mentality and, what is particularly important, political culture, has 'united in friendship' adherents of ideas that have for decades opposed each other.

Certainly, the Russian 'fundamentalists'' prejudice against the Islamic fundamentalists will almost never disappear completely. This would be simply impossible. The point that really matters to us in this case is that fundamentalism is not an exclusively Islamic phenomenon. It is present in one way or another in other civilisations as well – sometimes in a'distorted form, as it is in post-communist Russia.

Let us, however, revert to Central Asia.

The events in Tajikistan in 1992 revealed that, despite the potential strength of the fundamentalists they do not yet have sufficient resources and popularity to unite the Moslems of even one nation, to say nothing of those of Central Asia as a whole. The civil war in Tajikistan, in which the fundamentalists turned out to be no more than one of the belligerents, has demonstrated their inability to draw a majority of the population to their side and, what is more, to work for the formation of some kind of Islamic state, which is objectively their final strategic goal. It has also become obvious that the fundamentalists' slogans are often adopted by political adventurers, mafia networks and, plainly, bandits. The idea of fundamentalism, like the Islamic political movement, has been compromised. Somehow or other, fundamentalism on CIS territory is ever more frequently associated with dead bodies in the streets of Tajik towns, with the sufferings of tens of thousands of people, with the wrecking of a whole state, even though it is known for certain that it is not the fundamentalists who are to blame for that bloody drama, nor was it they who initiated it.

The Tajik drama provided the administrations of the Central Asian states, including Kazakhstan, with a powerful trump card in their struggle against the opposition, especially the Islamic opposition. The presidents of Uzbekistan and Kazahstan thus obtained a golden opportunity to point to their southern neighbours as examples of what an administration's 'spinelessness' might lead to. It is no accident that, precisely at the moment when the Tajik developments were at their peak, measures were taken in both these neighbouring states to ban the activities of Islamic parties and groups.

The civil war in Tajikistan ended in the defeat of the opposition coalition whose mainstay was the fundamentalists. In December 1992, virtually with the support of Russian troops, the post-communist bodies succeeded in restoring their control over Tajikistan. According to press reports from Dushanbe, numerous members of the crushed opposition, including PIR members, were victims of harsh reprisals. Thousands of people were shot.

And yet one can hardly speak of the final rout of the fundamentalist movement. There are reasons for believing that this was a temporary defeat and that Islamic fundamentalism has every chance of restoring its strength and of trying to 'replay' the lost war.

In future years, the Islamic movement will remain one of the most influential political forces in society. Besides this, one should not disregard the fact that fundamentalism will be nourished from outside: from Afghanistan and Iran. Even now one can already speak of mutual support and cooperation between individual fundamentalist groups operating in Afghanistan and Tajikistan. This is without mentioning the substantial Iranian influence on the inhabitants of the mountains and plains of the Pamirs.

Without indulging in futurological speculations, one can none the less presume, with a certain amount of confidence, that the growth of fundamentalist tendencies will have not only a direct impact on the alignment of forces in Central Asia, but will also somehow or other affect events even inside Russia. Two consequences are already evident: first, the strengthening of fundamentalist sentiments among Russia's Moslems and, second, growing emigration of the non-Moslem population from the Central Asian states, which will create, and is already creating, extremely complicated problems for Russia.

Notes

1. Gilles Kepel, *La revanche de Dieu*, Paris, 1990, pp. 25, 26.
2. *Programme and Rules of the Party of Islamic Rebirth*, pp. 6, 8.
3. *Al-Vakhdat*, 2 March, 1991, Moscow.
4. *Nezavisimaya gazeta*, 6 July 1991.
5. *Komsomolets Tajikistana*, 14 December 1990.
6. I. Makatov, 'Stepping up reorganisation of atheistic education', *Kommunist Uzbekistana*, Tashkent, no. 11, 1990, pp. 64, 65.
7. *Erk Demokratik Partiyasy Gazeti* (in Uzbek), Tashkent, December 1991, pp. 12–18.
8. *Megapolis-Express*, 16 January 1992.
9. Aron Atabek, *The Alash or the Kazakh Nation* (in Russian), Moscow, 1991, p. 12.
10. Khak (Islamic political newspaper), no. 2, 1992.
11. Ibid., no. 1, November 1991.
12. *Nezavisimaya Gazeta*, 18 May 1991.

CHAPTER SIX

NEW MOSLEM CENTRAL ASIAN STATES AND RUSSIA

After the disintegration of the Soviet Union, the ruling establishment of its former Central Asian republics found itself, as it were, face to face with its own social, political and economic problems. Their newly elected presidents had to map out domestic and external policies, comprehend their place within the framework of the new, relatively quickly formed CIS, and also define their attitude to the Moslem world. Naturally, the young Moslem states relied, not without reason, on Russia's aid and support. But on the other hand, because of several objective and subjective circumstances, this aid was rendered on a rather limited scale.

Besides this, Russia was seriously worried about the alignment of political forces in the Central Asian states and the activity of the opposition, including the fundamentalists, who seemed to be able to expect an increase in their influence now that the USSR had disintegrated.

None the less, however noticeable is the presence of the Islamic political movement in Central Asia and however great its potential, on the whole it is not this movement which determines the position of the 'new Moslem states' in the CIS. Nor is it the fundamentalists who determine their political orientation, even though – we will repeat this once again – the influence of the Islamic movement is sufficiently strong.

In the course of *perestroika* and subsequently, following the disintegration of the USSR in the autumn of 1991, power in the Central Asian republics remained in the hands of their former communist rulers – first secretaries of the local communist parties and the groups and clans supporting them. Even in Kyrgystan, where the young and energetic Askar Akayev, who has relatively little connection with the former top brass, was elected president, the parliament and local administration are almost entirely composed of the former communist *nomenklatura*. Only in Tajikistan did the new opposition forces, led by the PIR, succeed in participating for a few months in the governing bodies. Yet, in the end, the forces that held power in that republic before the disintegration of the Soviet Union managed to regain their lost positions and now the communists are once again in control of powerful levers of government there.

The confrontation between the post-communist authorities and their opponents has led to a civil war – dead bodies in the streets of Tajik towns, famine, flows of refugees, economic collapse and, even, a threat of disintegration of a state that was until recently quite stable. All this has demonstrated, as if under a magnifying glass, the extreme complexity of Central Asia's transition to . . . to what, exactly, the transition was to be made, neither the authors of this book nor, perhaps, most of the region's political figures, can definitely say.

In any event, the young Moslem states are yet to establish themselves within the CIS and to make their presence known in world geopolitics, having first chosen a suitable model of development.

The first year of their independent existence showed that the Central Asian republics of the former USSR were the least prepared for independent decision-making and, what is more, for independent action. It was they that were the most ardent champions of preservation of the Soviet Union whose formation, in the phrase of President Islam Karimov of Uzbekistan, had been for them an achievement 'gained through suffering'.[1]

On the other hand, among the new Russian leadership there was a marked tendency to view continued closeness with Central Asia as a kind of necessary evil. Speaking of Russia's attitude to Central Asia, Uzbek writer Sergei Baimukhametov sadly compared Central Asia with a 'faithful but hated wife'.[2] In Moscow, Central Asia was regarded as an obligatory partner and a 'necessary' ally from which, however, no assistance was to be expected since it was itself in need of assistance.

Are these views not, at least in part, the reason why the leaders of Russia and her two 'Slavic sisters', the Ukraine and Byelorussia, did not even notify the Central Asian republics of their intention to restructure political relations in the former USSR when they met not far from Minsk in December 1991, for they believed that the Moslems would remain at their side all the same? Thus it happened that the CIS was formed without the direct participation of the Central Asian republics, even though they subsequently welcomed its formation.

This action was described as 'incorrect' in Central Asia. 'Such isolation, not to say opposition,' wrote the *Turkmenskaya Iskra* newspaper, 'would be nowhere near the civilised standards of relations between states.'[3] Immediately after signing the treaty between Russia, the Ukraine and Byelorussia, on 12 December 1991, five presidents (those of Kazakhstan, Kyrgyzstan, Tajikistan, Uzbekistan, and Turkmenistan) met in Ashkhabad. At that meeting they decided on mutual coordination of their policies in case the Slavic republics acted again in the same way, without regard for the opinion of their Central Asian neighbours.

On the very eve of the meeting of the Central Asian leaders, President Saparmuryad Niyazov of Turkmenistan made a visit to Turkey. This was in a way symbolic.

The establishment of a fundamentally different state formation with an indistinct outline in place of the USSR, and vague prospects for their own future, compelled the Central Asian republics to turn their eyes towards the Moslem East which was following developments on the territory of the former USSR with undisguised interests.

The Central Asian republics, when they were still part of the Soviet Union, had begun to establish contacts with Moslem states, particularly with those that were ready to render economic assistance and grant financial credits. The countries with the greatest attraction for them included Saudi Arabia, Kuwait, the United Arab Emirates, Turkey, Iran, and Pakistan. The plans for enlisting their cooperation were fully in keeping with the idea of Moslem solidarity. Such cooperation was objectively becoming a 'bridge' which was to restore the broken ties between the Islamic world and its Soviet province.

For a short time, the Central Asian leaders developed something in the nature of euphoria about the scope and duration of assistance which they hoped to receive from their wealthy brothers in faith. Rather soon, however, this turned to disappointment, for seasoned Moslem businessmen from the Near East and the Arab world are in no hurry to invest heavily in the ruined Central Asian economy which, on top of everything, has retained such characteristic features of Soviet socialism as rigid centralised management, limited private initiative and absence of modern technology. The old afflictions have been aggravated by new ones brought about by clumsy attempts to make the transition to a market economy. Added to this is the political instability observable in several regions, and the fact that power in most of the republics is still held by yesterday's communists. All this is putting their Moslem neighbours, who sincerely wish to develop their relations with Central Asia but are in no hurry to take risks, on their guard.

Their interest in establishing close economic ties with Central Asia is further reduced in conditions of political instability. This is what happened in Tajikistan. Moslem businessmen, worried by the outbreak of civil war, practically suspended their economic activity in the republic. The financing by Pakistan of the construction of the Rogun hydroelectric power station was frozen, as were credits from Arab countries. This is the most vivid example of such suspension. The concern with which even seemingly commonplace 'disturbances', such as the student demonstrations in Tashkent in February 1992, are received in the Moslem world is well known.

One can understand President Islam Karimov of Uzbekistan, who stated sadly in February 1992 that relations between his country and Saudi Arabia 'cannot be described as fruitful'.[4] This statement may, on the whole, well be applied to the other republics as well. It should be noted that in general the extent of their contacts in the political sphere – between presidents and prime ministers – clearly exceeds the scope of economic cooperation so much desired by the Central Asian states.

Relations with Turkey

Perhaps the most substantial progress had been made in development of relations between the Moslem republics of the CIS and Turkey. The main reason for this success is that Turkey is the country which all the Turkic states of Central Asia have tried to take as a model for their development. In the winter of 1992, all the local presidents unanimously expressed an interest in the Turkish model. (Askar Akayev, President of Kyrgystan, said without beating about the bush that his republic 'chooses the Turkish path of development'.[5] In fact, it should be noted that the 'Turkish path' has been sanctioned by the Moslem clergy whose most authoritative representative, Mufti Muhammad Sadik Muhammad Yusef of Uzbekistan, believes that 'the Turkish path of development is congenial to us [Moslems]'.[6]

This stance was welcomed in Turkey whose prime minister, Suleyman Demirel, and other political figures, repeatedly stressed during their meetings with the heads of Central Asian governments that their country was ready to lend them every support. In describing Turkey's stance, *Newsweek* magazine pointed out that 'while Ankara still forcefully denies any political ambitions in the region, the outlines of a kind of Turkic commonwealth are beginning to emerge'.[7] Turkey is giving the Central Asian republics massive humanitarian assistance and has increased its credits to them. For example, Kyrgyzstan has been given US$75 million by the Turkish Eximbank for the development of its economy. Uzbekistan is to receive US$590 million for development. In 1992, 500,000 tonnes of grain credits were granted to Kyrgyzstan while Uzbekistan received 2 million tonnes of wheat. Joint Kazakh–Turkish, Uzbek–Turkish, and other ventures are being set up. Turkey is contributing to the development of infrastructure in Central Asia, which tallies with its own interests, since this facilitates future Turkish economic expansion. Finally, Turkey is actively entering the Central Asian information and publishing markets. In July 1992, the first Uzbek–Turkish newspaper, the *Zamon*,

Figure 20. Mosque Tilla Kolla (XVII c.), al-Registan, Samarkand

was launched in Uzbekistan. Turkey has also rented up to seven hours of broadcasting time on one of the local television channels.

The enthusiasm for the 'Turkish model', which is being encouraged by Ankara through aid, does not, however, mean that Central Asia today has the practical opportunity to implement it. The top, and particularly the middle, echelons of government in Central Asia have rather quickly become firmly convinced of the impossibility of reproducing the Turkish model in the local context. The difference between Central Asia and Turkey in terms of the 'starting point' are far too great and the burden of the 'socialist experiment' is far too heavy. (As Islam Karimov stated in 1992, the Central Asian republics' misfortunes are a result of attempts to 'teach them to jump over capitalism'.) The mentalities of the Turkic peoples, which seem to be so similar to one another, also differ in many ways.

In consequence the 'admiration' for the Turkish model is

increasingly combined with an awareness that it cannot be repeated and that only some of its elements can be used in conjunction with the Central Asian republics' own experience. 'We should not copy what other people have,' President Saparmuryad Niyazov of Turkmenistan casually noted one day. Apparently, most politicians in Central Asia are gradually arriving at this conclusion, while clearing for their peoples 'their own optimal path', as President Nursultan Nazarbayev of Kazakhstan put it.

A pragmatic trend is taking root not only with regard to the attractive Turkish model. The Iranian version has in fact been rejected. From the very beginning all the Central Asian leaders spoke in favour of forming secular states and – putting it mildly – took a critical stand towards Islamic fundamentalism.

Iran, for its part, is striving to strengthen its influence in Central Asia, but the shadow of Khomeiniism, even in its present-day, very liberal form, reduces the possibilities for Iranian penetration into *Ma Wara al-Nahr* (the old name of the area between the Amu Darya and Syr Darya rivers). It seems that certain commentators, particularly those in Europe and the United States, somewhat exaggerate Iran's opportunities when they speak about its competition with Turkey for influence in the Moslem region of the former USSR. Even in Tajikistan many politicians, fundamentalists included, are apprehensive about Iranian influence in the mountains and valleys of the Pamirs.

It is also interesting to note that Tajikistan turns its eyes, in searching for its own path, not only towards the world of Islam, but also, in certain cases, to the experience of the European countries. 'If the people and its intelligentsia and clergy choose a way which has stood the test of time and which will bring them peace', one Tajik publicist observed, 'this will result in forming a state in the heart of Asia after the fashion of Switzerland in Europe.'[8] Alas, most tragically, these hopes have not yet come true.

Russia as guarantor of stability

The search for their own way inevitably brings home to the new Moslem states the fact that they have many problems in common with Russia. Most of the local politicians, both those in power and those in opposition, are aware that their countries' ties with Russia, even if they are not to everyone's liking, remain a long-term stability factor and that their severance would be fraught with unpredictable consequences. It is also obvious that Russia's economic and military presence in the Moslem region is a guarantee of political stability. (This is perfectly understood in Europe and the United States where religious fanaticism today gives rise to much greater apprehensions than do the communists' successors.)

The Central Asian states have no intention of breaking their economic ties with Russia. They have signed a number of agreements with Russia in the military sphere which legalise the presence of Russian troops on their territories. This is the case in Turkmenistan, for example, where, according to a politician close to the president, the army will, under joint command, 'defend Russia's interests on its southern frontiers'.[9] Kazakhstan and Kyrgyzstan have no armies of their own, this function being performed by the CIS forces. The Uzbekistan president, meanwhile, signing a bilateral treaty with Russia in June 1992, said that 'without relying on Russia's potential it would be difficult for us and our neighbours to map out our prospects for the future and find the way out of . . . the grave crisis situation . . . We view Russia', he continued, 'as a guarantor of stability, peace and tranquillity, and of the inviolability of our borders. We are interested in this.'[10]

This idea was further developed at a meeting of the heads of Central Asian states and Kazakhstan held in Bishkek, capital of Kyrgyzstan, in April 1992. The striving for, strengthening and reforming of their ties with Russia remains a major (but, certainly, not the only) strategic line of their policies. And ignoring this stand by the Russian leadership would be a grave mistake.

Therefore attempts by certain Russian political analysts and the media to dramatise the situation and raise the spectre of the 'formation in the future of a superpowerful aggressive Moslem grouping that would include Pakistan, Iran and Afghanistan, as well as the former Soviet republics'[11] seem misplaced.

Formation of such an alliance arouses no particular enthusiasm in the rest of the Moslem world, least of all in Istanbul, which has more than once been criticised by Moslem radicals in Central Asia for its 'weakness' of faith, secularism and pro-Western orientation. Concern about the formation of such an alliance has been expressed in the United States and Europe.

Thus, Russia hardly needs to be concerned about the emergence of an 'aggressive Moslem bloc' near its southern frontiers; not to mention that its potential 'adversaries' are more concerned with settling their own, much neglected, home affairs. The point of view held, in particular, by the political analyst Akbar Rashidov, who observed that Central Asia, while being increasingly drawn into the orbit of Islamic politics, 'is becoming a transitional stage from the countries of so-called "hard-core" Islam (Iran, Pakistan) to more temperate Asian regimes'[12] seems to be more balanced.

But what is the attitude assumed by Russia itself towards Islam and its nearby Moslem neighbours?

After the formation of independent Russia, it seemed that the Russian leadership, having turned to the West and trying to prove Russia's political and cultural affinity with Europe, went as far as to push its relations with the Moslem world (which had always been one of the cornerstones of Russia's political interests and orientations), into the background. The Russian leadership gave the impression of being ready to return Russia to Europe even at the cost of changing its historically established geopolitical status which had in many ways ensured its status as a unique Eurasian power. It is interesting to note in this connection that it is precisely in the Moslem states of the CIS that attempts are being made to remind the Russian leaders of their predecessors' failures to 'join Europe'. 'There have been quite a few attempts at such modernisation [after the European fashion] in the history of Russia,' sociologists B. Aripov, A. Ilkhomov and I. Pogrebov from Uzbekistan said and then, citing the adoption of Christianity in Ancient Russia and Peter the Great's and Pyotr Stolypin's reforms by way of examples, they concluded: 'Each subsequent modernisation . . . usually effected by forced spurts . . . brought about natural resistance of reaction, arousing the dormant forces of conservative habits and archaic traditions.'[13]

Russia coexists with the world of Islam in three dimensions. The first one is represented by the Moslems residing inside the Russian Federation itself; the second is represented by the Moslem states of the CIS; while the third includes the countries of the Near and Middle East, as well as more distant Moslem regions.

For all its differences and contradictions, the Moslem world has a tendency towards integration and in many cases it may be regarded as a rather monolithic conglomerate capable of upholding the interests of each of its members. The Moslem *umma* (community) in the sphere of politics is a reality, particularly so on a regional level; like the idea of Moslem brotherhood, it can have quite a tangible effect on the formation of a general Moslem political consensus. Hence it follows that Russia's ties with the Moslem world in all the three dimensions are closely interdependent. And Russia's relations with the Moslems of Central Asia inevitably affect its relations with the states of the Near East.

Moslem politicians and mass media, for their part, keep a close watch on how Moscow treats their co-religionists, making their own judgements on the subject.

At first, the predominant feature of Russia's official stand towards the 'nearby' part of Moslem world was short-term pragmatism, which was effective within a relatively limited time-scale but which in the final analysis hampered the elaboration of a foreign policy strategy.

Among the Russian top echelons, there was also perceptible indifference concerning such a question, decisive to the former Soviet Moslems, as the choice of the path of development; for it was erroneously believed that this would have little effect on the desire, common to all the Central Asian states, to preserve their ties with Russia.

In general, Russia's stand in respect of the Moslem world was not unlike the Euro-American approach to the Moslems, the essence of which is to stimulate the process of modernisation of traditional society after the European fashion, its secularisation and the gradual renunciation of traditional standards of behaviour at every social level in politics. This may be judged, in particular, by the example of Russia's attitude to political Islam in Central Asia and Transcaucasia and in the Moslem regions of Russia itself.[14]

In Moscow it was believed that in Central Asia Islam was, or rather had to be just a religion; and most Russian politicians refused, and now refuse, to view it as a legitimate, independent, political force. Besides, politicised Islam or fundamentalism is associated, in the minds of the Russian Democrats, with Imam Khomeini or Moslem extremists in the Near East who constantly destabilise the situation and have an extensive list of assassinations of their political opponents, including Egyptian president Anwar Sadat and Algerian president Mohamed Boudiaf, to their 'credit'.

The Central Asian ruling circles are trying to frighten their counterparts in the other CIS countries with fundamentalism, representing themselves – not without reason – as the main bulwark against 'religious fanatics'. The presidents of the new Moslem states are aware that it is the fundamentalists rather than the uninfluential Democratic opposition who are their closest and most dangerous rivals.

Problem of Christian Slavic minorities

The question of the Russian leadership's attitude to the followers of fundamentalism is particularly important since it will be, and already is, directly related to the status in a Moslem region of Christian Slavic minorities that are clearly apprehensive about the prospects for social and political models being established in that region which are similar to those in other Moslem states. This is without counting the threat to their lives and well-being that may be quite real under conditions of political instability that may grow into civil war as they did in Tajikistan.

The Russian government is giving some thought to the problems of the Russian minority in the Moslem republics. Indicative of this are Russian foreign minister Andrey Kozyrev's meetings with representatives of the Russian communities in Uzbekistan and Tajikistan (where Russians constitute up to 10 per cent and 8.5 per cent of the populations respectively) at which they were told that 'the problem of the Russians whose destiny it was to find themselves outside Russia certainly worries the President, the government and the Supreme Soviet of the Russian Federation'.[15] This statement, made by the head of the Russian foreign policy department during his visit to Dushanbe, is fully applicable to the Russians living in other regions of Central Asia.

The 'Russian question' is given attention by most varied forces in the Moslem regions. And not a single serious political party or movement aims to strain relations with the local Russian and other non-Moslem populations. Thus, the Uzbek newspaper *Narodnoye Slovo* noted with pride that 'the unswerving policy of civil peace and concord being persistently pursued by the authorities and every public organization with the slightest pretensions to responsibility produces quite tangible results in Uzbekistan'.[16] Characteristically, the local Russian-language press even advocated a kind of 'Russian Uzbekistan patriotism'. This is quite natural, for many Russians living in the republic, as well as in other parts of Central Asia, regard that 'part of the world' as their native land and, if they emigrate, find it difficult to settle in their historical homeland.

It seems that a substantial share of the Russians who have settled in the 'land of Islam' will not, in the next decade, leave what has been home to them for many years. (This is with the exception of Tajikistan, from which more than 200,000 Russian refugees have fled because of civil war.) Concern about Russian Christian enclaves in the Moslem world is bound to become one of the major areas of the new Russia's foreign political activity. Moreover, the presence of the Russian minority may in a sense become a restraining factor in the way of possible nationalist or religious-fanatic ambitions. A seemingly paradoxical situation is developing: under the system of centre–province relations established in the USSR, the Russian minority was a 'hostage', as it were, of the provinces in their confrontation with the centre. Now the former provinces, having become sovereign states, have themselves to take care to ensure normal relations with their influential neighbour. And it has become all the more essential to them to maintain their reputation with Europe and the United States, for which the observance of human rights, including the rights of

Figure 21. Minaret and madrasa Khodja al-Islam (XX c.), Khiva

ethnic minorities, is one of the decisive criteria in the rendering of economic and other assistance. At the moment, however, this is only the authors' hypothesis.

Since the spring of 1992, the positions of those who recognise the importance of Russia's position in the Moslem world and the significance of Russian–Central Asian relations are gradually strengthening. In the spring of 1992, a certain change in Russia's approach to the Moslem world began to be seen. Indicative of this is Andrey Kozyrev's 'long-awaited', although belated, visit to the Gulf countries and the intensification of Russia's political activity in the 'Moslem area' of the CIS.

On the other hand, President Yeltsin of Russia is still striving to consolidate the CIS (in whose formation he himself had a hand), which, in his opinion, tallies with Russia's interests. In this regard his stand, coincides, in the main, with that of the leaders of the Central Asian republics, who are actively supporting the idea of forming a political, economic and military alliance. The results of the meeting of the head of the CIS states held in Tashkent in May 1992 are also indicative of a *rapprochement* between Russia and the Central Asian republics, although the photograph showing Karimov, Yeltsin and Nazarbayev together ascending a stairway, which was published on the front page of *Izvestia* on 15 May 1992, can hardly be called a symbol of the political situation. The Tashkent summit was followed by a whole series of bilateral negotiations and treaties between Russian and the Asian republics of the former USSR. It seems that Russia and the Moslem states, apparently to their mutual satisfaction, have found the line of conduct which presupposes both preservation of close ties and acknowledgement of each other's mutual interests.

In the meantime, Islam and the Moslems have already, for quite a long time, been in the field of vision of the forces that are in opposition to the Russian leadership, above all, the so-called National Communists, who are more or less consistently 'developing' the Islamic factor in two opposite directions, both at the same time. Firstly, they are 'initiating' Islam in their struggle against democratisation of society, which, in their view, is contrary to both Russian Orthodox and Moslem political culture. Quite significant in this connection is the fact that *Den* newspaper, an organ of the so-called spiritual opposition, offers its pages for publication of excerpts from writings by Ayatollah Khomeini. Another Moslem who has long become popular with the National Communists is Iraqi Foreign Minister Tariq Aziz, an opponent of Islamist Iran.

Before the disintegration of the USSR, the National Communists (and also the party functionaries and journalists who were close to them) welcomed the Central Asian republics' striving to preserve the Soviet Union and described with sentimental affection the political stability and relative economic well-being that were observed there, contrasting the idyllic picture of Central Asian life with Russian chaos.

All this was presented, on the one hand, as the result of following the local, and in particular the Islamic, traditions, which were shown to be guarantees against any radical social and political changes and, on the the other hand, as the consequence of people remaining faithful to the socialist ideals.

This turning to the Moslems is fully in keeping with the Eurasian motifs advocated by the National Communists, who, in the name of preserving or, rather, restoring the empire, declare their support for the alliance of the Slavs and the Turks, the Moslems and the Orthodox Christians.

Yet these very same National Communists express grave apprehensions about the threat posed to Russia by the Moslem world capable of acting to the detriment of its interests. A. Rudakov and S. Shilovsky, adherents of this point of view, fear the formation of some 'Islamic strategic consensus' which could 'claim world domination in the interests of the planet's demographic majority'.[17] And the *Nakanune* newspaper frightens the reader with the possibility that in 'the Asian republics there may happen things which will cause Russian blood once again to flow like water'.[18]

And now last but not least: National Communism is afflicted with an imperial grandeur complex, which will always hinder its advocates from abandoning the model of inter-ethnic relations of the 'senior brother-junior brother' type to which they are accustomed, as well as the firm conviction that Russia has a special mission which has made the neighbouring peoples, including Moslem peoples, happy.

And yet, what is Russia to expect from the Moslem world? And what is the Moslem world to expect from Russia?

In answering the first questions we proceed from the fact that, firstly, the Moslem world as a whole is favourably disposed towards Russia, wishing to see it as a stable and strong state, and has no intentions of entering into any kind of confrontation with it.

Nor do the CIS states, where the diversification of economic relations and foreign policy sympathies appear to be combined with the desire to preserve stables ties with the Russian Federation, aim to strain their relations with Russia. Today not a single organisation or movement, including the Islamists, calls for a break with their northern neighbour, even though they subject it to harsh criticism. This certainly does not, however, completely rule out the possibility of conflict, which is not unusual under present-day conditions, particularly since possible conflicts will hardly be in the nature of 'Russian–Islamic confrontation'.

As for Russia, everything seems to indicate that its ruling circles have already begun finding the necessary key to their approach to the Islamic world, both within the framework of the CIS and in the Near and Middle East. And Russia's traditional ties with the Moslem peoples must become an integral part of the system of new geopolitical relations.

Notes

1. *Izvestia*, 1 May 1991.
2. Ibid., 8 May 1992.
3. *Turkmenskaya Iskra*, 25 December 1991.
4. *Narodnoye Slovo*, 21 February 1991.
5. *Nezavisimaya Gazeta*, 3 January 1992.
6. *Narodnoye Slovo*, 14 January 1992.
7. *Newsweek*, 3 February 1992.
8. *Narodnaya Gazeta*, 4 January 1992.
9. *Nezavisimaya Gazeta*, 16 June 1992.
10. *Narodnoye Slovo*, 2 June 1992.
11. *Megapolis-Express*, 19 November 1991.
12. Ibid., 11 April 1991.
13. *Narodnoye Slovo*, 12 February 1992.
14. A. Malashenko, 'New Russia and the world of Islam' (in Russian), *Svobodnaya Mysl*, no. 10, July 1992, pp. 28–36.
15. *Narodnaya Gazeta*, 10 April 1992.
16. *Narodnoye Slovo*, 25 April 1992.
17. *Russky Vestnik*, 25 April–5 May 1992.
18. *Nakanune* (Russian newspaper), March 1992.

BIBLIOGRAPHY

Agzamkhojaev, A., *The Soviet Multinational States* (in Russian), Tashkent, 1962.

Ayni, S., *Materials on the History of the Bukharan Revolution* (in Russian), Moscow, 1926.

Bartold, W., *On the History of the Arab Conquest of Central Asia* (in Russian), Moscow, 1964.

– *The Kirghiz* (in Russian), Frunze, 1948.

– *Twelve Lectures on the History of the Turkic Peoples of Central Asia* (in Russian), Moscow, 1968.

Benigsen, A., and Lemercier-Quelquejay, C., *Les musulmans oubliés. L'Islam en Union Soviétique*, Paris, 1981.

– Sultan Galiev. *Le pire de la révolution tiers mondiste. Les inconnus de l'histoire*, Paris, 1970.

Bogoutdinov, A. M., *Essays on the History of Tajik Philosophy*, Stalinbad, 1961.

Caldorola, Carlo (ed.), *Soviet Central Asia. A Religious Limbo*, Berlin, 1982.

Gasprinski, I., *The Moslems of Russia* (in Russian), Simferopol, 1881.

Institute of Islamic Civilisation, *Islam and Problems of Intercivilisational Interaction* (in Russian), Moscow, 1992.

Litvinsky, B. A. (ed.), *The Tajik. A Primeval, Ancient, and Medieval History*, Moscow, 1972.

Olcott, Martha Brill, *The Kazakhs*, California, 1987.

Pierce, Richard A., *Russian Central Asia 1867–1917*, Berkeley and Los Angeles, 1960.

Polyakov, S. P., *Traditionalism in Modern Central Asian Society*, Moscow, 1983.

Ro'i, Yaacov (ed.), *The USSR and the Muslim World*, London, 1984.

Saidbaev, T. S. *Islam and Society* (in Russian), Moscow, 1978.

Sreznevsky, I. I. (ed.), *A Miscellany of the Russian Language and Literature*, St Petersburg, 1881.

Tolstoy, S. P., et al. (eds.), *A History of the Peoples of Uzbekistan* (in Russian), Tashkent, 1959.

Vambrey, A., *A Journey over Central Asia* (in Russian), 2nd edn, Moscow, 1867.

Velikhanov, *Selected Works* (in Russian), Alma-Alta, 1958.

Zenkovski, A. Serge, *Pan-Turkism and Islam in Russia*, Cambridge, Mass., 1960.

INDEX